I Say Tomato

Patrick Swayze Makes a Medium

Jodie Archer, Ph.D.

First published by Sidonia Press, 2017

Copyright © 2017 Jodie Archer

All rights reserved.

ISBN: 9781973429890

For Linda
1948-2013
Mother

"I have the meanness and the passion to say to hell with you. Watch me. You watch what I pull off."

> —Patrick Swayze to Barbara Walters, January 9, 2009. From TV special *Patrick Swayze: The Truth*, filmed during his battle with pancreatic cancer.

CONTENTS

Chapter One	7
Chapter Two	21
Chapter Three	33
Chapter Four	40
Chapter Five	48
Chapter Six	60
Chapter Seven	70
Chapter Eight	79
Chapter Nine	92
Chapter Ten	104
Chapter Eleven	118
Chapter Twelve	126
Chapter Thirteen	136
Chapter Fourteen	147
Chapter Fifteen	159
Chapter Sixteen	168
Chapter Seventeen	178
Chapter Eighteen	188

CONTENTS

Chapter Nineteen	195
Chapter Twenty	200
Chapter Twenty-One	211
Chapter Twenty-Two	228
Chapter Twenty-Three	243
Chapter Twenty-Four	251
Chapter Twenty-Five	261
Chapter Twenty-Six	278
Chapter Twenty-Seven	287
Chapter Twenty-Eight	296
Chapter Twenty-Nine	305
Epilogue	320
Song List	323
Acknowledgments	325
About the Author	329

CHAPTER ONE

The taxi driver pulled up and verified the building's address from the scrawled writing on the paper in my hand. Hot rain was bouncing off the crumbling tarmac.

"This looks like it," he said. "This area is where all the students are. Not a palace but you'll live," he chuckled. "You students don't give in. Study, study, study. Even in summer! I can take you back to the airport!" He was in a breezy mood for this hour in the morning. I had just got off a redeye flight from San Francisco.

"I've come this far," I said.

The taxi driver carried my suitcase to the front door and pressed on number two. A male voice answered, and the driver nodded and wished me well.

I stood there in the early light. I was early by about fifteen minutes.

Eventually, the door opened, and a young guy ushered me into my summer home.

"Take a look around," he said. "Jodie, right?"

"Right. Thanks for offering me your place." It had been Craigslist. "It was really hard to find somewhere."

"You're English," he said. "I didn't realize."

"Yes. I have just been in the US for almost three years."

He nodded. "It always is busy for summer season. Cornell runs a lot of summer programs in all different things. Campus will be full."

"Ah. I only knew two weeks ago that I was coming."

"I'll bring your bag in," he said. He hadn't offered me his name yet and I couldn't remember it from the last-minute emails.

"Thanks. When are you leaving?"

"I'm packed and out," he said. "Just came by to pack the last of my books up and let you in."

I went inside and walked around the small one bed apartment. The taxi driver had warned me.

The floor was stained, the bathroom taps were thick with chalk, and the thin, dark curtains were slouching off their hooks at one side. Through the slatted metal blind at the bedroom window, I could see the rain forming puddles in the car park. People would be able to park close enough to hear my breathing at night. The thought was a little scary. The doors were old and thin. I didn't really like the idea of being here alone.

In the kitchen slash dining slash living room there was a small grey box sofa, an extraordinarily large fridge freezer even for someone now used to the US, and various mismatched plates and glasses. There was a TV from 1995 and a large stain in the carpet that may have been a Bolognese. I could picture the cursing when it had flopped off the plate.

"These shelves are full of stuff I didn't know where to put," said the guy, pointing to bookshelves at the kitchen end. I remembered he was doing a Ph.D. in engineering. The shelves held an open bag of barbecue coal, rusted tongs, various loose batteries and papers, and a flashlight. "In there's where the trashcan goes," he gestured to a closed closet door with his head. "But be sure to leave the lid closed cuz of ants."

"Alright," I said. I wasn't sure it was.

"That's everything then," he said. He had a nice, Christian, hopeful smile and ballooning khakis. "There are lots of bookshelves in the hall around the corner, you might have seen."

I nodded.

"You won't need much other than those if you're doing the School of Criticism and Theory. It's intense."

I nodded again, feeling a sinking feeling to my core. Me and my enthusiastic ideas.

"Great," he said. I thought perhaps his name was Chris. In the top left corner of the window behind him was a house spider in a web that looked older than he did. Thankfully, I'm not scared of them.

"Do you like being here?" I asked him. "I mean, Cornell and things?" From the tiny airport to the apartment block in the taxi, I'd seen only run-down big houses, big green empty garbage containers still left outside, and little sign of energy other than the hydropower falling monsoon style from the sky. Suddenly, I wanted to cling to him and ask him to take me back to the airport in the old estate car that was parked just outside. I'd done this on impulse. But I was tired from a stressful academic year, and looking at the crack in the ceiling I thought that maybe a summer of rest in California might have been the better plan for me.

"Sure," Chris said. "Ithaca's ok." He smiled cautiously. "There's a nice café up the hill. People hang out. There's really nice scenery if you like to hike on the weekends. There is the famous vegetarian restaurant. It'd hard to get far without a car unless you get to know the bus schedule out of town. Mostly I just work." He looked more bashful than proud about that. "Ph.D., you know? I think you'll like it. You'll have a good time."

"I hope so." I didn't want it to get awkward. "Well, I love to hike between classes at Stanford. I didn't sleep on the flight. I'll probably have a rest then go and explore."

"Be sure to. Thanks for the check. Leave the place clean after the quarter ends and I'll send the deposit right back to California." He gathered his things.

"No problem." I smiled.

"Why does an English person do a Ph.D. in English in California?"

I'd been asked the question at immigration in San Francisco airport about five times, every time I flew back from visiting home.

"Money," I said. "Lucky scholarship money."

He nodded. "Good for you. Everything ok?"

"Oh yes," I say, looking around. "Yes, thank you. It's great. Enjoy your summer away."

He scribbled a contact number on a takeout flyer and was gone.

"Shit," I said as I dragged my bags to the bedroom, flopped down on the double bed, and heard springs. "Shit."

When I'd slept and the rain had stopped, I had a shower and went straight out. No-one would call me a cleaning freak, but a house is a home and this was a dump. There were no sheets on the bed. There were no pictures on the wall. There was not much natural light. I felt cold on the inside, being tired and unsure of myself with no creature comforts at all.

I was in one of seven apartments. Outside the main door and across the carpark, I saw I could go up or down a long road. I'm terrible at geography, and in fact most things involving spatial awareness. I learn land by walking it, then walking back, then repeat. I had accepted this in myself, and I tried not to make a sarcastic comment when my family still suggest—even though I was twenty-nine by then and some things don't change—that I learn to read a map. Those who map everything miss the adventure.

There were no real clues as to where I was. The street was wide and tree-lined with large houses side-by-side that were likely once grand and now housed students looking for cheap rents near to the university. The driveways were lightly scattered with empty soda cans and potato chip packets. The cars were all ten years old or more. The dilapidation was a little bit sad.

I'm better at research than maps, but I had not had chance to research this town near the Finger Lakes in upstate New York. I was half-way through a Ph.D. in literature at the time, and just the week before I flew to Ithaca, I had passed a three-hour oral exam after nine months of stuffing myself with books until I felt like a foie gras goose. It had been the second of three grueling oral exams on the way to a doctorate, and the work had been so intense that I hadn't looked up to think about this trip until the night before I was leaving. Consequently, all I knew was that the summer class started tomorrow and I was due in a building named after a benefactor at 6pm for welcome drinks.

Right then, it was eleven fifteen and the air already held the kind of humidity that felt interfering. It was such a different heat from dry Silicon Valley. Still feeling woozy from the night flight, I made it easy for myself and went downhill towards the main town. The landscape is all hills: up to campus side and down to the non-student side. I was used to walking them, since I grew up in Yorkshire.

I ended up on the edge of downtown Ithaca. I bought random groceries, cleaning supplies, a small vase and candles. I bought a slightly sad looking bunch of mixed flowers and shoved them under my arm. They'd do: it was Sunday and I was no longer in an all flowers at all times metropolis. By the time I got back to the apartment, I was clammy, my hair had been thrown up into a rare bun on top of my head, and the brown paper groceries bag was torn almost in two. The open living room was in shadows. Despite the bright sunlight of this June day, the room remained in greys. I tried not to think I had made a mistake.

It was supposed to be somewhat of an honor that I was in Ithaca for the next six weeks. I had won a scholarship to be there. I'd written applications, taken an interview, ignored the jibes of my friends at Stanford who asked me what could be worse than going to summer camp for literary theory. Eating worms, they'd suggested, or maybe cutting off my own hand with a butter knife? I had rehearsed my justifications for them and my husband, Edward. It was a prestigious course at Cornell. People from all over the world went, some of the best professors in the field. They had listened over a pizza, not particularly impressed. I was hoping to settle on a dissertation topic that I'd enjoy for the next three or four years of my life, I'd said. And besides, it could always look good on a résumé in a field where competition for a job was getting irrationally intense. They still didn't care. It seemed perfectly rational to be on the wrong coast of the US for the summer. Besides, it made me three thousand miles closer to my mother in England, who was thinking about flying over to New York for a few days. They had all rolled their eyes and let me get on the plane. Edward understood. He had just finished an MFA and meeting the cost of living in the Bay Area was a constant pressure. We had to say yes to whatever might bring me a good academic job when I graduated.

    I arranged the flowers and put them on the edge of the counter. I put a bottle of white wine in the fridge, and a gallon container of milk. The size of everything in mainstream America is built around the expectation of family. No small cartons of milk for lone expat students. No great variety of English tea to go with it. And yet the US is the only place with real opportunity for a humanities student. There was funding there for the liberal arts that doesn't exist anywhere in the world. My time at Stanford was all expenses paid. My time at Cornell was all expenses paid. This apartment might not have been what most women would like to call home, but it wouldn't go on a grad student loan thanks to the fact that wealthy Americans, unlike the British, were still pouring money and support into the humanities subjects at the top schools. They saw, some of them at least, that science is not the only religion—not the only perspective on the world and its inhabitants worth considering. I was grateful for that, I truly was.

That's what I was thinking about as I was scrubbing gunk off the bathroom sink. I was wondering if gratitude was blinding me. I had left a job in London publishing to accept this scholarship, and after a year I had started to feel like it hadn't been the best choice. I hadn't been wowed by an environment of buzzing ideas and inspiration for a better world, as I had hoped. People mostly towed the line in the library, rarely coming forward with a maverick statement. Three years in, I had experienced much more of that. I had attended seminars and written papers and put on ten extra pounds that I could see in my face as I scrubbed the mirror. But I had committed now. Edward had moved over from England. We had made some good friends. But there I was waiting to read for another solid six weeks, to open another thirty years of reading more books and delivering more papers. I was wondering if this was right. It likely took moving to the other coast to let me dare to really think hard about whether I still wanted it all.

It took me fifteen minutes with a scourer to shift that hardened spat-out toothpaste in the bathroom, and then I went behind the sofa and try to fix the blind.

Once I'd cleaned, I unpacked summer dresses and jeans, too many for the closet, all packed last minute and without much thought. I'd need to buy a sweater or two. I'd forgotten my hairdryer. Thankfully I did remember my makeup bag, which I'd left on planes before. I'd been flying to academic conferences to speak, and I'd been flying when I could to see my mother, who was alone in England with a long-term blood disease. It wasn't unheard of for me to rush off a plane to make a connection and not check if something had fallen out in the overhead.

I put a bit of make-up on to brighten me up a bit. I'm blonde and the fair eyelashes are not my best feature when I'm tired. Mascara and blusher helped a bit.

It was only when I sat to text Edward, to ask him if he'd draw me some pictures and send them for the walls, that I rested for a few minutes in the living room. Sitting still, I felt something. I looked around. I felt there was a presence in the place. I wondered if it was an old house converted. Or if perhaps someone had died there. I glanced around, scanning. I didn't feel nervous. I just also didn't feel alone.

I had seen and felt ghosts since I was three or four. England is full of old houses and if a nice house were for sale, my mother or her friends used to send me inside and up the stairs to see if it were haunted. I always saw them, and didn't think much of it. As a little girl, I was scared to talk to a ghost, but I could see them and even once heard a call. None had ever hurt or upset me and it had been years since I had felt all that much.

As a child, it would start with a prickle up the back of my spine. I had the same sensation in my new summer home in Ithaca, but the prickle was warmer. Friendly. I hadn't thought much about my sensitivity for twenty years. I only ever really thought about it if I had time alone. Some members of my family and some of my friends were well aware of it, but no-one had ever encouraged it. I was surrounded by empiricists, and so I never developed my receptivity with thought or application. Mostly, I felt nervous to be singled out and turned away. I didn't want to be bullied or branded a strange child.

It was true that mediumship had been brought to my attention haphazardly but fairly consistently over the years, mostly by total strangers. My mind was flooded with those memories as I sat and rested that first afternoon, not yet ready to climb the hill to acquaint myself with Cornell. Sitting in the peace and quiet of this new and stark room, all those memories gently came to the surface.

To date, four strangers, each in different places, had come up to me and told me that they believed I was a medium or a psychic medium. Once was near home in England at a Christmas party. I was fifteen. The lady who told me was a medium herself. She said it was something to pursue one day, despite the environment I'd been born into, which was upper middle class and focused on traditional education. She said from her own experience she wanted to prepare me that it might come. One incident was in New York, where I had lived for several months while working in publishing. A dark-haired woman chased me a full block and told me my light was on and I had to know from a stranger that I was a medium. I took it in but mostly dismissed it. I was not having mediumistic experiences. Another person told me in New Orleans, of all places. A stranger in a metaphysical book store that I had happened to stroll into. I'd been in Texas and New Orleans at the time finding out, thanks to work experience with a Texan attorney, if I wanted to pursue a career in the law. The fourth time was during a tarot reading at home in England. I had asked about getting into Cambridge, and which subject I should study. Spirit is calling you, was how the lady had put it. She'd said just to pick a subject and go with the flow. So, I focused on an academic career that started at Cambridge and moved me to California. I mostly dismissed all these spiritual comments, and made little of the random occasions in my life that I'd definitely seen ghosts. My heart and mind had been with other things, and it had been that way for many uninterrupted years. I hadn't yet spotted a pattern, which was that every time in my life I had put myself on a possible career path—with the publisher in New York, or the lawyer in the American Deep South—some message came through from a spiritual person telling me to rethink, or else to not get too involved.

Since Edward was not in Ithaca, I instantly reverted to pre-cohabitation practices. I replaced the meal I would have made with half a bag of cherry tomatoes and crackers dipped in a fresh pot of hummus, shoved straight in my mouth from the fridge. I sat with a mug of tea for thirty minutes at the desk in the hallway-turned-study. I looked closely at the contents of the fat brown envelope which had been delivered from Cornell. A class time table. Daily from nine to noon. Afternoons left to reading. A list of people in my class. They were from the best universities in the world, and from European universities I had never heard of. And the reading list. It was hefty and it was intense. I knew some of it, which would buy me some breathing space. But this wasn't genre fiction. It was philosophy and theory. Baudrillard. Derrida. Foucault. Heidegger. Kant. The unpronounceable names said enough.

    I found myself distracted as I read. I turned over my shoulder then looked back. If anything, the presence around was strangely comforting. I was nervous about being in Ithaca. There was expectation on me for high performance in an area I was uncertain was for me. My professors wanted a good report and a high-flying thesis topic. My husband wanted success for both of us in California so that we could stay. We still had a green card to fight for.

    I could see or hear nothing in the place. There was just something in the air that soothed me. I imagined it to be old and wise enough to make little of my inner turmoil about my future, or else strong enough to guide me out of my own possible drama.

    This summer would be my testing ground.

CHAPTER TWO

There is a lot of loyalty in Ithaca. People young and old walk around in T-shirts that read "Ithaca is Gorges". The slogan is in shop windows and bumper stickers, available on baby rompers and candy bars. The man who congratulated himself on that pun has probably made a lot of money. The ubiquity of the phrase seemed somewhere between joyfully boastful and a little bit desperate, confident but not quite confident enough that we'd notice the gorgeousness of Ithaca all on our own. In affection for the memories that came there, I'll say I noticed, but that was still a week or two away.

That first evening, I went and found Cornell University. It stands at the top of a long sweaty hill, still and grey and beautiful. With picturesque gorges, of course, a bit dried up now but impressive enough that you can still get the original point if you're feeling generous. The campus has natural waterfalls and a pretty lake. I said some hellos at the welcome drinks. I listened for half an hour to the different universities people were from and what they were interested in studying. Then I left and took a stroll. I needed to orient myself with a good walk.

Ithaca is really an undergraduate town. Cheapish restaurants mostly, lots of launderettes, and a few budget clothes shops, all with the T-shirt. I found a fun Chinese restaurant with fortune cookies for dinner, and the place everyone goes for dessert, hard to miss as it stands on the corner of the pedestrian area with a display full of twenty versions of chocolate and cream. I sampled one, which was delicious. I would survive in Ithaca.

I managed to make a bed from new cheap bedding, but I spent the night twisted in the sheet. It was sweltering. The next morning was so hot and humid that by nine o'clock my hair was stuck to my back by nine, and I slid around in my flip-flops. Non-locals couldn't stand it. You could see that the minute they got up for a new day they were tired again, broken by heat and those massive hills. I saw one younger student buy a water bottle, have a sip, then think again and pour it over his head. Everything was intense and close: the stare of other graduate students, the air, the demands for attendance at guest lectures and afternoon study groups. The supplementary reading lists and highly-strung demeanour of other younger graduate students. I started to feel grateful that my apartment didn't have much natural light or any flat mates.

I started my course at nine on Monday morning. It was the end of June. There were four large groups, perhaps a hundred people in total, and my group would meet each morning for three hours to discuss readings from the afternoon before. The professor was a good woman, quirky, still passionate from the heady days of the sixties and seventies about intellectual theories that were supposed to deconstruct the world. I listened to her explain her background. She had a passion inside that I thought she might never get to bring out. She felt that philosophy and theory, rather than practice, might change the culture we live in. In a less grand setting it might be called "talk over action".

My fellow classmates, whose ages ranged from twenty-three to thirty-four, were serious, fierce and eloquent in their opinions. From the first moment, they threw opinions into the classroom as a fencer might work around a room: stab with the rapier, duck to flee, stab again. Graduate students are competitive but mostly try to hide it, all peacocking knowledge at half plumage, all aware that there are very few jobs out there, even for the best. It was not unlike my days at secondary school, when I'd see girls surreptitiously roll their waist-bands over twice more and put on lip gloss when we were near the boys' school, only to deny it to their friends.

I watched, listened to most of the three hours of talk, but didn't say anything. There were characters in the room determined to shout down other ideas, and others who were quiet and more brilliant, sitting like silent spiders in a web, waiting for some inadequate and unsuspecting being to get caught. The interaction was almost exhausting. We were debating the basic philosophies underlying the course. There was no forgiveness in those gunmetal minds, which should have carried some logo of German engineering. My peers were good-humored but without compassion, as though compassion in an intellectual arena were a weakness. I made friends with the guy to my right, Paul, whose eye contact told me he was thinking more or less the same. He was Canadian and wrote on a notebook to me, "Only an hour to go!"

Three days later, I had already got into the bad habits of picking from bowls of leftovers while sitting at my desk, skimming pages of text, knowing enough just to follow along. I should have allowed myself a break but I hadn't.

I was reading theories of postmodernism when I reached for a highlighter in my handbag. My handbags are a bit shameful, since I usually prefer very large ones and never clean them out. They are full of everything, designed to carry anything from the laptop and books to a change of clothes or a friend's wallet or a random purchase. In a creative writing class, I once had to write a list of about the contents of any one thing that would tell a story: a bookcase maybe, or a database. Perhaps a heart. It could be about anything that contained other things. The rules were simple like in all good writing. Look at what's there and put it down without lying. Tentatively, I chose my handbag. I tipped its secrets all over the floor for the exercise. Some things inside were lost and suddenly recovered like my California ID. Some were illustrative like a pair of flat shoes and an empty notebook. Some were plain nasty like old gum in receipts and a really pink lipstick called Bombshell. It was a queasy set of revelations, looking through that bag, a bit like looking under harsh light into one of those magnifying mirrors that show you every moment you have had too much pleasure under the sun. I even found Thai money and a receipt for a pedicure in New York in 2005.

Rooting around in the bottom of my handbag, my hand couldn't feel the shape of a highlighter, but I did find my old pendulum tucked into a seam. It was a much happier find than a highlighter. I hadn't seen it for a about two years, likely because it had been lost in this seam with a load of crumbs. It's a dull, opaque cream rock on a chain, a moonstone. I still have it. I bought it along with an amethyst one for my grandma when I'd randomly noticed them in a shop. She had liked pendulums, typically used for dowsing. I put mine on my desk like a talisman and carried on reading in preparation for the next day.

On Thursday, I woke up with an idea in my mind. The idea had urged me out of sleep early, and it persisted all day without rest. I could barely concentrate in class, but by now cliques had already formed and my friends would fill me in. I had Paul on my right and Mike on my left. Along with two other girls and a third guy, we were little group who had started a habit of having lunch together. Each of us would then go to the library or home until about seven or eight, when someone might text to meet for a drink.

Everyone was working hard. But after class on Friday, I rejected lunch offers and bought a long ruler and a small pair of scissors. I was following the details of this idea that had been with me all day. I went home, took some paper from my printer, got one of the mismatched plates from the drying rack and laid it face down on the page. I drew around it, feeling somehow urged. I cut the circle out, not particularly well, wrote A at the top and M at the bottom and guessed at evenly spaced dots between those two letters to make twenty-six. I didn't do that particularly well either, I thought when I looked at it, since X, Y and Z were squished a bit close. But it was fine.

I drew a large black dot in the middle of the circle and ruled a line from it to each of the letters. I was left with something like an alphabet bicycle wheel. I had never seen it done before, but I had woken up feeling like I was meant to do this strange thing.

I picked up the moonstone at the little kitchen table and held it over the dot in the bicycle wheel. It hanged on its metal chain about six inches in length from my thumb and finger. I would have been the first out of the door if something felt wrong or uncomfortable. But it didn't. I just wanted to know what would happen if I saw this gentle urge through.

Straight away the pendulum moved. I held it as still as I could between my thumb and index finger, watching. It moved in gentle circles that got wider, spinning out towards the circumference. I just watched, saying nothing. While I couldn't feel any change around me, inside my heart had jumped.

The pendulum stopped at the centre, with a dead stop, almost impossible to understand from the physics I knew. Then it started to swing over the A, right over the ruled line I had drawn. Then it adjusted and moved forward and backward over B, then C and D. There were couple of swings over each letter, then a stop, and then the same at a new angle, a bit like pendulum warm up exercises.

I could not believe what I was seeing. I was mind-blown. It was the first time I thought that phrase really was the right one. Even though I'd just clearly presumed this was possible in the act of cutting the circle and marking the letters, it was really not possible either. This thing was moving directly over the marked lines, even over the ones with miscalculated angles, right out to each letter. E, F, G. Some intelligence that moved it knew these angles. There was something graceful about it, something quite hypnotic, and though my heart had quickened now, I was still unafraid. I asked myself if that was really true, since it was eerie to watch this movement that ignored basic science, but really the answer was an honest no. I was not scared. I was dealing with my own subconscious here, I reminded myself. Or at least I thought I was. What else could it be? I was fascinated.

"Is my name Jodie?" I asked. It moved over Y and then stopped still. I got up and grabbed a notebook and a pen, thinking maybe I'd get a word.

I went back to the wheel and held the pendulum again. It swung to H and then stopped. Then I. That was odd and brought a strange sensation. I'd describe it as a feeling that comes when you've found something you've both wanted and not wanted to find. Like the ghost in the attic, or your lover's secret diary. I looked around the room slowly, like you do if you hear a creak. Nothing, of course. "Hi?" I said aloud, mostly to myself.

Then something happened that changed me. Poised between my fingers, the pendulum swung with the ease of a dancer over the letter N, then O, then N, then N, then Y. It stopped, its movements flawless.

I was stunned. This was a miracle. Nonny was a word I did not need to write down. Nonny is a word I'll remember as long as I live. It is family alternative name for Grandma or Nana, used in my family and among my Austrian cousins. It is the nickname of my grandma and no other grandma that I know other than her sister, who also chose it over Granny.

I didn't say anything. My brain had not caught up. The stone moved again, fast and confident. I was starting to tingle. I-L-O-V-E-Y-O-U. Dead stop. I was amazed, wordless, and felt just rushes of emotion. Then the moonstone spun fast in my hands and I just got a real presence of knowing all around me, in some part of the air.

"I love you," I said quietly, somewhere between statement and question.

I became nervous but I didn't know why. Was this my grandma? She had died earlier in the year. I was sure I was not influencing the stone. It was one of those things you trust from the get-go because you know your own motives. I was not moving this thing. I didn't want to move it. I don't know how I could like that, at these sudden angles, with these abrupt losses in velocity as it stops.

I didn't know what to say. Was she there?

The pendulum swung forward and back and then brushed over M, O, then R and E. More? I thought. I didn't know what more meant there. More what? I tried to slow my rushing mind, but it started guessing anyway. One of Nonny's favorite and identifying words was "moreish", which she used in reference to chocolate truffles and Bailey's Irish Cream. But it was moving too quickly to stop and think clearly.

And then it came. From my mind or my heart or heaven I didn't know, but without wasting one second this moonstone pendulum spelled out with crystal clarity: T-H-A-N-A-L-L-T-H-E-T-E-A.

I cried. I didn't really feel it coming but tears started falling down my face. I hardly dared ask out loud, it felt so ridiculous and so hopeful and so naïve all at once.

"Nonny?"

I was wiping my cheek on the back of my left sleeve as my right hand was gripping the pendulum. It spun fast, out and wide almost horizontal to the table and in circles. Then it carefully touched on each of the letters that spelled I-N-C-H-I-N-A.

"And all the coffee in Brazil," I said aloud. She had written it at the close of all the letters she had sent me over the years.

"Nonny?"

For the next six hours, I sat at that table with the pendulum in my hand and only moved once to get dinner. As the moonstone moved over the letters with effortless precision, never one mistake, I become more and more confident that I was really speaking to the spirit of my late grandma. I was not even totally sure I believed in an afterlife where relatives could visit us wherever we were, but she was impatient to debate. It wasn't a theoretical issue. She was there, being it. I wrote each letter down and responded aloud, every word like a little blessing. Her character was still there, the way she would say things was still there. She was still there. I adored Nonny. As the time passed I felt that mutual love return, no longer lost to the past. As she slowly wrote sentences to me, I felt her gifts of connection and protection, ongoing love, straightforwardness, and some wit. Just like her.

It took ten minutes, letter by precious letter, but she told me she had seen her funeral and had heard my eulogy for her. She said it made her teary. I recalled looking up from reading the eulogy and seeing my cousins and her brother in tears. She was much loved. The memory made me teary sitting there at the kitchen table. She told me she knew I had written an essay on her for all the family, which I had. She was even able to recite a scene, as though she's watched me compose or read it.

This was real. I could somehow feel her smile in that room—it is hard to explain but I felt emotions in the space around me. I tried not to analyze, but instead to just let it be, in its moment, ethereal. It was the most special gift to have my grandma back for those hours.

It got very late and before I gave in to sleep, she gave me little messages for my mum and her sister and, knowing her daughters well (Christine especially), she patiently offered me long lines of information to verify with them. I would need more to tell them than they could expect, and she asked me to call them and repeat it. She wanted them to know she looked over them, happy to be where she was and with family. With her own parents again. She told me to light a candle when I used this pendulum, to draw the good, to be protected by the light in my own heart, and to keep going. She said that she was proud.

I was choked. I didn't want to put the pendulum down. I didn't want her to go. She told me this connection was going to be part of my life. I had to learn. I noted it tiredly. I was emotionally drained and mentally exhausted from class. I had class up the hill at nine. It was late.

I told her I loved her, that I would cherish this evening, and that I was so grateful that she had come to me, especially as I had never got to say goodbye to her. I was speaking out loud, sad but happy.

The pendulum was still a second, listening. Then it moved.

T-H-E-R-E-I-S-N-O-G-O-O-D-B-Y-E.

CHAPTER THREE

I had a bit of a background with pendulums. Not much of one, and never before had I made a lettered circle and contacted the dead. Nonny had been the centre of my experience with pendulums before she died, and perhaps it followed that I had the urge to pick mine up when she had wanted to make contact.

She had always kept a hand-made pendulum in a pot on her sewing table. It was just a silver point from an old fancy zipper on a long thread of cotton. She called it her dowser. I can remember as far back as when I was six or seven, she would show me it. Half-serious and half the entertainer, she had let it hang still between her thumb and index finger while she asked it questions. If it moved one way, forward and back, it meant yes, and the other way meant no. She only asked it yes and no questions, and sometimes held it over the pulse of her left wrist. She once told me you could even tell the sex of a baby if you held it over a swollen belly, but we didn't have a pregnant lady to try it on.

I was never sure if she quite believed in the prophecy of her pendulum. She liked to experiment with it, and she tried sometimes to reach into the realms of divination.

After a second or two of hanging there, her makeshift pendulum would start to spin in circles, and as a child I would walk right over and peer at her hand, practically with a ruler, to see if she was moving it. I didn't like to be fooled. With my eye on her she'd ask, "Is Jodie going to do well at school this year?" Her question was always something like that: Jodie and school. Nervously I'd watch it change path, switching from the circle of hello as she understood it to the forward and backward swing of a yes. I believed her that she wasn't moving it on purpose. I couldn't find any evidence that she was doing in my investigation, and when I questioned her she promised. So, I accepted it and did do well at school.

This continued over the years. She didn't mention it more than one or twice a year, but I was aware it was there in her little pot. She'd write to me often and if she thought I was worried about something, she would send me a card saying something like "I asked my pendulum and it said you will get in to Cambridge," or, possibly to back up a point she'd been hinting at without spiritual intervention, "It says this boyfriend is not right for you and you will break up with him." She liked it when her pendulum justified her own poorly veiled opinions, especially if they were regarding a young love interest that she thought would distract me from school and family. She would end her letter always with lines full of Xs, and Os for hugs, and that phrase "I love you more than all the tea in China and all the coffee in Brazil." I loved that saying, it was just so her in its original charm. She had said it again ten years later as she hugged me in the corridor of her nursing home before I ran for a flight to San Francisco. It would be the last time I ever saw her alive.

Mostly she was right with her predictions hobby, but sometimes my mum would observe it suspiciously when it was saying just want a grandma might want it to say. "No Linda," Nonny would insist. "It is telling the truth! I just happen to share that belief!" She would turn back to her friend on the string. "Now what shall we ask about Linda today? Any new men on the scene?" She'd dangle it, waiting, and then look up, rolling her eyes to heaven. "Still no! What is wrong with you Linda?" My mum wasn't interested in another new man, but Nonny was always interested in a companion for her.

This was the background behind my decision to buy Nonny and I proper pendulum each when I came across a display of them once in a shop that sold crystals and gifts. I chose two, not knowing why I'd selected for myself that most bland and unattractive of stones—the opaque bone coloured moonstone, other than when I'd picked it up it had started to move. The lady in the shop told me that many people believe pendulums give access to channeled energies, but whether they are from areas of the mind we are not conscious of or an outside source like an angel she didn't know. She said that when you pick up a pendulum you should definitely ask if it's the one for you. That sounded a little mad, given they were rocks on chains, but to prove her point she had asked me to look at my own hands, which had a pendulum dangling from each. I had been distracted by her but now I looked, and was surprised to see them moving in opposite directions, one forward and backward, the other side to side. It was strange, since I wasn't moving. The moonstone, apparently, was saying yes to me and the amethyst no. She was encouraged in her mini lecture. On her instruction, I had held the moonstone and asked, a little aware of myself I'll admit, if my name was Jodie. It said yes. Was my name Fred? No. I was enthralled at how quickly it moved and how effortlessly it changed direction. Was I a woman? Yes. Obviously. I did the same with the amethyst asking about Nonny, and took it to her as a gift.

That would have been three or four years before I got to Ithaca, in June 2010. The September before, Mum had asked me if I thought Nonny would make her hundredth birthday, who had been ninety-three then. How on Earth did I know? I really hoped so.

I found my pendulum, just to see what it said. It swung no, she will not, no massive insight perhaps since a hundred is still rare. But then with yeses and nos, forward and back, and left to right, it had said to me as I guessed months and days that she would die on May 8th of the following year. I don't even know why I asked, or how it occurred to me how to do it.

I had dismissed this news at the time, not quite a believer in the Grim Reaper's pre-scheduled visit, but of course it had stayed in the back of my mind as these things tend to. Thankfully, May 8th came and went. Nonny was totally fine in health, Mum said when she called on that day, but the one unusual thing was that Nonny started saying a nice man had been sitting in her room since the morning, smiling at her. She didn't know him, but when she followed him to her door he disappeared into thin air. She had no sign of dementia, but still no-one in the home believed her. Knowing her, hearing her insistence, we just found it strange.

On May 12 I got a call in the middle of my class at Stanford. For once I'd left my phone on by mistake and I just knew I had to take it. It had been my Mum on the end of the line, teary.

"You were four days out." Nonny had died in her bed.

I sat and reflected some more in the windowless corridor that was my new study. I rolled the moonstone in my hands, held it out and it was still. Despite the prediction, I had been shocked by my grandmother's death, and deeply upset. We had been very close. She'd had pneumonia a year earlier and we were told by the doctor she'd likely die. I'd told a friend who was interested in alternative healing, and she'd advised me to picture her with green healing light all around her, and to send her white light too. I mean, I was in California now, land of the new age and home to the hippies. The suggestion struck my English background as out there. But so what? I did visualize for a few minutes, and then went to our chalkboard at home. I drew a stick figure of a woman in a triangle skirt with curly grey hair, drew an arrow pointing to her saying "Marie Durham/Nonny" to avoid confusion, and a colored a big green ring round her. Then I added a white arrow right into the top of her head to signify light going into her. I kept it in view all week. Edward chuckled at me. But it was sending the light in some dimension wasn't it? I felt helpless. She lived.

In May though, I was in grief. I bought a white candle like I do when I hear someone has died, dedicated it to her and sat in front of it. I erupted in tears. I didn't like to cry much back then, having that instilled sense (wrong but instilled) that it's a bit needy and pathetic. But this crying was involuntary and I thought of her and sobbed. I got a photo of her, put it with the candle and cried again. I just could not stop it flowing, mascara streaked down the backs of my hands. I'm quite a silent crier but I spoke to her a bit, I think, between breaths.

Later I thought about that prediction. The death had somehow still shocked me, like it remains shocking when someone dies who was terminally ill. The finality that comes between one second and the next, and the instant absence, cannot be prepared for in the heart, even if the rational mind is ready. Part of the ongoing shock was the prediction, just on a pendulum by someone as inexperienced as me. Should I have taken it seriously and flown home to be there? Should she have died on the eighth? Do we all have a date we are meant to die? And if we do, who knew that information , who also knew about my pendulum?

This kind of thinking was me, not really. But that night in Ithaca I allowed my mind and heart to go into the unknown with innocence and without the typical chastising I gave it as a so-called rational academic. I sat with the pile of reluctantly read books, my pendulum now spinning lightly in my hand. Perhaps the idea of my stubborn left-brained empiricism was starting to wear a little thin. It must have been. Who was that disappearing man in Nonny's room before she died? I couldn't help but wonder about it. The moonstone started to swing.

CHAPTER FOUR

The next morning, I woke early before class and picked up my moonstone. I looked up its properties online. It was supposedly the stone that will show you what *is*. It is the crystal of telling the future, of divine inspiration and of good luck. It is believed to have occult and magical powers, given by moonlight. In India it is quite sacred, and can only be displayed on a yellow cloth. One website told me that if I was drawn to it in a shade of white instead of blue, rainbow or any other color of moonstone, I was probably ready for it to facilitate spiritual growth. If only there were a handbook to go with the seemingly random intuitive things we sometimes do.

That day, I was very surprised to get the name George spelled out for the first time. He was my paternal grandpa, who I wasn't particularly close to, and who I'm sure would have thought of mediumship and pendulums as baloney. He died when I was eleven. He told me he was aware of my successes at school and some other personal bits of family information that I hadn't known. I immediately emailed my mum with a few questions about him, and she wrote back that yes, what I was saying about him had been right.

I told my grandfather I was surprised he had come through because I thought my father's side of the family were very scientific and empirical in their beliefs. He said something kind and diplomatic, along the lines of we don't always know something until we experience it. You might deny an afterlife until you are in it, he said. He also told me to take mediumship lightly, and beware of family concern over it. He told me to trust my education. I had fought hard for it.

It didn't surprise me at all that I had grandparents on either side of my family with different implied attitudes toward my sudden ability to hear from them, if only via a pendulum. I would have hardly called myself a medium, using a tool like that. Both sides of the family had been soft, but they nevertheless demonstrated what I had grown up with: a scientific, intellectual and atheistic father, and a creative mother who has more open to spirituality in its broadest sense. I could feel both pulls in me, and always had. The contrast was obviously a few generations old.

The walk up to campus from the apartment took roughly twenty minutes. I had to be in the classroom a bit before nine. The route I took went past the student area of town up the hill, into the bottom gates of the university and up alongside a steep tree-lined drop looking onto a waterfall. The top of that hill lead to another, the third long slope of each morning. When the terrain finally flattens there is the big clock tower and a large oval of handsome and austere buildings, each proud and silent like Etonian men. There are lawns between the buildings, perfectly cut, two or three well-spaced trees, the ancient sort of trees which know things and which people capture in expensive black and white photographs. The colors are sophisticated and educated: ivory not bright white, muted greys, and soft terracotta. It is impressive, built around the words *respect* and *tradition*. It is one of the best educational institutions in the country.

But it felt to me as though no-one has stood on those wide paths for a hundred years and really filled their lungs with air and breathed. I found it graceful yet somehow quietly stifling, like great aunts or mother-in-laws. It was a place that could shelter me for fifty years and I'd die among its heritage and beauty, knowing I had never really lived. On the way to class that morning, I wanted to run down the center of the lawns and scatter wild poppy seeds. I wanted something feminine and organic there, in this place that said "old male pride". It longed for something unkempt and natural. Soft. I found those qualities only in the view, which was Cornell's perfect compliment. It was high enough to look out for miles with a two-hundred and seventy degree view, and it looked down over haphazard patterns of woods and towns under a massive blue skyscape. The situation up the hill and amidst the waterfalls gives Cornell its character, and its appeal.

The class room we gathered in each day was old-fashioned and unmodernized, like the ones at Cambridge. There were none of the drop-down panels, multi-screens and ceiling spotlights of Stanford. There were black chalkboards, grouped desks and old chairs, and evens some broken ones around despite the financial endowment there must be to support the campus. It reminded me of England and perhaps it was meant to, since I felt just the same when I once visited Harvard—it felt like England, not as a native knows it but as it is stereotyped. The was a snobbery in the shabbiness, implied aristocracy and breeding. There was also a snobbery against the West Coast schools, which were considered too shiny and new.

I listened in class to more abstract theories of art and discussions of Kant. I listened to conjecture about the possible meaning of every last clause.

But it was summer and I didn't care.

I drank an iced tea in the sun, then went inside to avoid the highest heat of the day. I picked up my pendulum and my letters, hoping to speak to Nonny. I hadn't called my mother with all the details yet. She had been working all week, and I'd been waiting to call her on Friday evening or Saturday morning. Perhaps Nonny would add something to her messages. But the pendulum surprised me. It didn't say Nonny, and nor did I sense her presence. I got the letters P-A-T-R-I-C-K. It meant nothing to me. I put the stone down to think about it and came up with nothing. I picked it up again and it remained still.

One thing I did know is that I didn't know a Patrick.

I did some chores, still thinking and feeling vaguely worried. I picked the chain up again and its weight was still. Nothing. Where had they all gone? I called Edward and asked him if we knew any Patrick. He said he couldn't think of one. I hadn't told him about the pendulum yet. Our calls were about friends, later summer plans, and whether we could afford a trip to England. Besides, I had to tell my mother first. I felt right to wait and tell her.

In the mid-afternoon, I felt distracted from reading. I picked the pendulum up again. Again, I just got P-A-T-R-I-C-K. It didn't budge beyond that. I was frustrated and put it down, and went to meet Mike from class in a coffee shop for an hour.

Finally, I got hold of my mother on Skype. She looked drained.

"What are you doing?" I asked.

"Ironing."

"Can you turn the TV down please?"

"Sorry I must be going deaf like Nonny! It's just on in the background."

"What's on?" I asked.

"Some documentary about Hollywood stars. I'm half watching it with a glass of wine and the ironing. The biography channel has a new one every day at the moment."

She asked me about Cornell and I told her I was just starting to get into the course and that I was tired.

"You look it," she said. "I can't believe you're going to be reading all summer. Go find some new friends!"

"I have to tell you something," I said.

Mum burst into tears with my news of hearing from Nonny. I read her every line from my notes. I told her things they had said to each other when Nonny had been in her nursing home. I told her the colour of a jumper Nonny had bought her on a shopping trip to a local outlet. I had never seen it. I told her about how they'd witnesses a scrape of a car in the supermarket carpark while I was in California. All tiny and seemingly insignificant things, but they were things Nonny had chosen for me to write down.

"Do you remember these things happening?" I asked my mother.

"Yes. Every one."

"I know she was here," I told her. "I wrote pages!" I recited things then that Nonny had witnessed after her death. These were things that had occurred around my mother. They were things like a squabble she'd had with a friend, and a blood draw that apparently she had been tearful about. "You never told me you've been crying about the blood tests," I said. She had to have one every two to three months.

"There was just one that scared me," she said. "I didn't want to worry you."

My mother was known as a strong woman. Not a tough cookie character; she was sweeter than that. But she wasn't known to crumble either. Looking at her, I wondered if Nonny had given me these examples to warn me to pay more attention. I had no idea there was a squabble with her close friend or that the blood tests had changed. She had likely kept it from me because I had been under the pressure of exams. Suddenly I was very concerned.

"Why were you arguing with your friend?" I asked. "That's not like you."

"Oh nothing. Just her approach to doctors. All doom and gloom."

"Mum, is there something you are not telling me?"

"No!"

"Has there been a worse diagnosis?"

"No, I promise. No big deal. Just sometimes I feel more tired. The blood results go down and up, and when they are down a bit everyone panics. It's been like this for years. Really."

I looked at her, not very happy. I was her only child and she was single. We depended on each other for a lot.

Her surprised tears turned into a chuckle. "I can't believe my mother is spying on me from Heaven and has come all the way to America to tell you about it!"

That made me laugh too. It was just exactly what she would have done had she still been alive.

"Well she obviously is spying on us all!" I said.

"You better behave then, Goody Two Shoes," she said.

"You could go to a medium if you wanted to talk to her," I said.

"They are too hard to find over here! I don't know of one. Besides, it seems like I can just ask you."

"I don't think I'm a medium. This isn't real mediumship," I said.

"Still," she said. "It's a bit spooky. I feel comforted actually to think of her still around."

I was pleased to hear that. I missed my mother, and didn't like being away from her for months of every year.

"Do you know a Patrick?" I asked.

"No."

"Did Nonny?"

"Not that I know of, no," Mum said. "Why?"

"I keep getting the name."

She shrugged. "Can't help you there, Sweetheart. Go get some rest now."

"You too."

When we hung up I felt a weight leave my heart. The presence of an afterlife was new to me. But it did comfort me to think that we might be overseen by the people who had loved us. Even if I would never walk around naked, use the bathroom or have sex ever again.

CHAPTER FIVE

That weekend, I tried to escape into the outdoors and do some good hiking, but I kept getting a strong, visceral pull to pick up the pendulum again. It was a pull from the belly, a call from the heart. It was so strong that it became physical, like a dragging sensation. I resisted my spirit for all of Saturday, and when I finally surrendered my life changed irrevocably.

What happened was this.

I picked up the pendulum again. It swung rapidly. I went to get the letter wheel, still the same basic piece of paper, and decided to just be receptive. I really wasn't afraid of the idea that someone who has died still has consciousness. In fact, it made some good sense to me. I didn't worry about dark spirits. Luckily, I felt immune to those horror films that suggest the dead are terrifying entities. I didn't have that state of mind. But I also didn't believe that people die and instantly become perfect angels. I did what Nonny had told me to do, and I lit a white candle.

Sure enough I got the name *Patrick* again. Knowing that I had a limited tool here, and that it might be frustrating for anyone trying to communicate through it, I switched to yes and no answers. A more seasoned clairvoyant medium would have had a field day watching this scene of my life. They would have been able to see and hear. But I can only offer you the story as it was.

This is the script from my journal. I wrote it day and night in Ithaca.

"Are you a spirit guide?" I asked.

Yes.

"Have you been my guide since I was born?" The pendulum swung no. I felt a presence close to me, and was sure this was the same presence I had felt when I moved into the apartment. I could identify it now at my back.

"Did you die a long time ago?" I asked, aloud. I don't know why I was conditioned to think of spirit guides as having died hundreds of years ago.

No.

"How long ago?" I said, then interrupted myself. "No, I mean, that's hard to answer with a stone on a string. Ok. Did you die in the 20th century?" It was really this level of patient pidgin spirit connection at that stage in my life. If I did have the gift all those strangers had told me about, then I had suppressed it fairly young, perhaps because it hadn't been accepted. It was a case of re-waking the gift and accepting it as part of myself. The connection definitely was not instant.

I must have looked a picture, talking aloud, sincerely staring over letters on an old pine table. But I had been trained to be patient with research in any area, so I continued.

There was a *no* to the 20th century.

"21?"

Strong swing to yes. I could almost feel a smile. Or perhaps I should say I felt a smile behind me and almost allowed myself to verify it.

"Are you English?" Perhaps this was a distant family member, or a friend of a friend.

No.

"Are you American?"

Yes. Again, the stone moved with swiftness when the answers were positive. I felt like I was being encouraged.

You know that family game where you have a name stuck on your forehead and you have to guess the identity using only a few questions? This was not unlike that game, and I wasn't mentally on the right tangent at all.

"What did you do?" I asked. "Sorry!" I was about to apologize for not asking a yes/no question, but the pendulum was moving over the letters in my right hand before I had time to vocalize it.

With proficiency, the pendulum swung over A, then C, then T, then O, then R.

"An actor?" I wrote the letters down. "An actor?" My mind went to theatre. There was some theatre in my background so that was the association. I know it sounds short-sighted now, but I just wasn't honing in to target at all. Why would I in this situation? I was perplexed, but still felt patient.

"Have I heard of you?" I asked.

A pause.

Yes.

"Called Patrick?" I said aloud. I was still drawing a blank. Have I told you that I am about the least celebrity proficient person under forty you could ever meet? I didn't own a TV at the time and hadn't had one for years. I never read newsstand magazines. I spent days and nights in books and conversation about different things with my friends. Edward and I watched films on DVD with a projector against a plain white wall in our house, and we tended to watch in a series we set for ourselves. Classics for a month or two. Then just one actor's work. Then adaptations. I didn't know my Kims from my Britneys from my Jessicas.

I felt that heat at the back of neck you feel when you are likely about to put your foot in it.

"Famous?" I asked. I was nervous to ask in case I was really about to make a fool of myself.

K-I-N-D-A.

If the air can laugh, it laughed at me right then.

"An actor in what?" I was tingling from head to toe. I felt nervous. I couldn't rationalize it. I had butterflies from nowhere. Why would a kinda famous actor be in this apartment wanting to talk to me?

M-O-V-I-E-S.

The pendulum had started spelling it out before I was really concentrating on it again. This actor had worked out this tool and how to use it.

I imagined my best friend saying "*Obviously!*" She was much more in tune with pop culture. She'd say, "Actor? American? Movies, you idiot!" She was American herself, and would be loving this.

I can only describe what I felt then like this. I felt vague pressure at my back and at the shoulder of my right arm. I felt warm, safe, but still vaguely nervous. Something inside me was pounding, signaling to me. Perhaps my spirit again, but I couldn't hear my spirit then. If I could, I wouldn't have been sitting in Ithaca reading for an entire summer when everyone in my life was telling me that it wasn't the best idea.

I can liken this inner signaling I felt to having a big finger at my solar plexus pointing to my left shoulder. In words, it was a voice calling *Notice! Notice! This is an important moment in your life plan!*

I knew this fated feeling already and I also didn't want to know it. I was still too ready to rationalize intuition. When I had met Edward in a shared job interview, we looked into each other's eyes and ran in the other direction. We both recognized feeling like the meeting had been pre-planned somewhere beyond our reach, like we already knew each other from somewhere. We felt fated. Being stubbornly free spirits at the time, we didn't want to recognize it. It felt like being told what to do, and we preferred to be a pair of wild horses. It took a work environment to bring us to heel, where we finally acknowledged each other and followed the flow of what had seemed meant to be.

We had to spend some part of our lives together: we knew it.

I didn't know what was happening in that moment in Ithaca or what I had opened the door on. But I felt that fated feeling in my stomach. I could feel a treadmill of my life kicking into motion, and I wasn't sure I wanted to get on it. I didn't have enough details. How I had trained my mind to keep control and to want control!

I started stalling. I didn't have a name, but I was pushing to get the name away. If an actor had turned up, I would have to look into it. I knew myself. I might threaten my success in the Cornell class with distraction. But at the same time, my curiosity was at its height. I thought I might ask just a couple more random questions.

The pendulum was already moving.

"A movie such as what?" I asked. "Maybe I'll have heard of it."

A-Y-Z-E.

They were the letters I caught quickly enough to write down. They are big in a page of my journal of that time. The pendulum was flying.

"Hang on, hang on." I was in the habit of writing the letters down as they came and then I was separating them into sensible words. I looked at the letters I had written. Then I said, "Y-Z-E? What the heck is that? That is not a word. It's nothing. YZE." It looked like the end of the alphabet, just random letters. Perhaps I should put the pendulum down and leave it down. "There is no movie with YZE."

S-W-S-W-S-W.

I added the letters to my page and a penny dropped. I looked at the page again. Yes, I felt more than a little bit embarrassed.

"Swayze?" The pendulum started spinning like mad. It nearly fell out of my hand. "Patrick. Swayze? Huh? Patrick Swayze?" I looked at my page, and yes, that was indeed what it said in black and white. "Patrick Swayze! Shit!"

Was he dead? I didn't think so.

"Is Patrick Swayze even dead?"

I got a strong *yes*.

"Are you serious? He died?"

Yes.

I couldn't find any words for what I felt. It was an odd sensation. Talk about being on the spot. There was real surprise muted by total bewilderment. I felt no fear, but my heart was racing. My spirit was lurching again, trying to get the attention of my brain. It was telling me that I knew and also did not know this was going to happen. It was telling me to concentrate a bit more on my sensitivity. Had I or had I not told a couple of people before I left for Ithaca that I had kept waking up feeling I was going to meet someone important? Well, yes, I had. I had to acknowledge that those statements had been coming out of my mouth during the past few weeks. But in my journal, I didn't get a lot further than writing a string of *?!?!?!?. Patrick Swayze?*

I held the pendulum still in my palm as I wrote, stopped, thought, and got nowhere. I hadn't been a fan of Patrick Swayze. I hadn't thought of Patrick Swayze in years. I didn't even know he'd died.

"I don't get it," I said. "Patrick Swayze?" Let me be honest with you. This was the strangest thing I had ever heard. "Patrick Swayze in the living room? Am I supposed to just believe this?"

My back was tingling like crazy. I remembered the feeling from visiting my godparents' house and encountering their friendly resident ghost on the stairs twenty years prior.

What do you do when you are a rational, sensible human adult and something totally crazy and multi-dimensional happens to you in broad daylight? I suppose you run away and ignore it or ask questions. I asked questions.

I held the pendulum over the letters. They just gave a *yes*.

"But why?"

W-H-Y-N-O-T.

The atmosphere in the room was alight. I didn't know a good enough answer.

"Where were you born?"

T-E-X-A-S.

For no particular reason, just trying to come to terms with this Patrick Swayze idea, I asked, "And die?"

"L-A."

I picked my phone up and called my best friend. The one who knew celebrity world better than I did. "Hi!" I said. "Don't ask but is Patrick Swayze dead?"

"Yeah," she said. "Why?"

"No reason."

"Don't you ever, ever buy *People* magazine?" She was in disbelief.

"No. I didn't know you did."

"It's just around, Jodie. In the world! He died last year."

"Oh. That's sad. Ok. Can I call you back later?"

"Sure," she said. "Are you alright?"

"Yep. Just wondered. You know about these things."

"Okay. Well, speak soon."

"Hang on. If he were dead, would it be totally unbelievable if he were in my apartment on this course in Cornell?"

She had always been less think, more laugh than me. She had always been spiritually inclined where I had been intellectually inclined. That is one reason why I liked her. "No!" she laughed. "It's hardly impossible! He's probably trying to save you! Or get through. Or wake you up. Maybe he's trying to get you to recognize that you are way too much in the head."

"Ha. Ha. Ha." I said. "It's not that bad."

"Yes, it is! You need to downgrade the excessive

school work. Look, I don't know. But you can find out. You tell Patrick Swayze hello!"

"I am being serious," I said. "Really."

"Well if he's in your house and it's him then at least look into it."

"Really?" She was more into this kind of thing. I had never given it much thought.

"Actor to spirit guide? What do I need a movie star spirit guide for?"

"My girl," she said. "My girl. Are you kidding me? Who cares what for? For goodness sake, stop always caring from your massive brain. Care from your heart. Care from the possibility of it."

"Okay."

"Oh, and as your bestie, can I just say something? Patrick Swayze? Darn!" The "darn" was pure American accented appreciation. "Congratulations! I think you just won the spirit guide lottery."

"Yeah, maybe," I said. It was still computing but I could see her point. Finally, I started laughing.

"Thank you! It laughs." She was always encouraging me to live lighter, with less dense thought. To accept life's conundrums instead of questioning them. "The guy from *Dirty Dancing* though?" I said. I was not so out of the picture that I didn't know who he was. "Showing up to be my spirit guide?"

"You are far too . . . closed," she said. "Too academic. Just sometimes be. He knows you can see the ghosties!"

"No, only you know that. And a few people who knew me when I was about seven." I said.

"Apparently not!"

I was silent. "Ok, ok. Well just find out and let me know!" She laughed. "The stuff that happens to you is just crazy! You're one of those people."

We hung up. I was alone again in a room with a presence that might or might not be the late actor Patrick Swayze. I kept quite still, with my phone on the table

That actor standing or sitting or just *being* right there in my awful little rented kitchen slash dining slash living room in Ithaca? With the stained carpet and the spiders? Oh, Lord! Just picturing it was something else.

"Ok," I said, holding the letters. I would have to be cool here, or straightforward at least. "Why are you my guide?"

I was staring at the moonstone, cautious but transfixed. Not fully trusting. Perhaps he and I both were. I could think of no personal connection to anything I knew about this actor, which was not much at all. But the answer came fast and assured, no beat missed. I wrote the letters down.

T-O-H-E-L-P-Y-O-U-M-A-K-E-A-N-A-M-E-F-O-R-Y-O-U-R-S-E-L-F.

"Huh?" This was making no sense at all. "What kind of name?" I was a professor in the making, sort of, with no name really likely. Certainly, I was not an actor, not since I was a kid and wanted to go theatre school. I shrunk at the thought. I felt unusually wordless.

"Well thanks, Patrick Swayze." It came out deadpan. I felt rude. "Sorry. I'm a bit surprised." My brain was laughing at me. But what could I do? I said, "Ok, Patrick, a name doing what? What would you like me to do?"

R-E-M-E-M-B-E-R-Y-O-U-R-S-E-L-F.

Remember myself.

A-N-D-W-H-A-T-Y-O-U-C-A-N-G-I-V-E-T-H-I-S-W-O-R-L-D.

I supposed it was true that I had got a bit stuck in mental worry. "How am I supposed to start that?" I asked. Did I dare to trust this voice, given only in letter by letter via a dangling crystal?

He signaled, simply: W-R-I-T-E.

"Write?"

E-V-E-R-Y-D-A-Y-A-N-D-I-L-L-S-E-E-Y-A.

The moonstone was still.

"Hello?" I said. "Hello?"

He had gone.

CHAPTER SIX

My first memory of Patrick Swayze was still vivid. This was not the first time he had burst into my consciousness without invitation, and not the first time I'd wondered if I were really meant to be there in the same space as him. It was not the first time I had felt both awed and slightly embarrassed by the closeness of his presence, and it wouldn't be the last.

The first time was not like this. It was not otherworldly or mediumistic, but looking back it was perhaps as strange a juxtaposition of him and I, the two of us shoved together like the dissonant parts of a Surrealist painting. From different worlds. Of course, it was a mediated meeting then as it was last night; we had never physically looked eye into eye or touched hand to hand in a formal hello. The first time we crossed consciousness, the introduction came not through a pendulum in New York state, but through the desperate wails of my mother and her sister in a living room in remote Yorkshire. Whooping and cooing might be more adequate words as they jived—literally jived, Mum the girl and Christine the boy, the only dance they knew—around the space in our house that I'd been told was for grown-up behavior.

It would have been about 1987 or 1988, no later because we had moved not long after my parents' divorce. So, I must have been six or seven, serious but inquisitive and full of good humour they tell me, and sometimes quirky: a kid. We had a white detached house then, symmetrical like the ones you draw at school. It had a big living room, or so it seemed at the time, with an open real fire grate set back into the wall, beside a small mahogany elephant and his friend, the rhino. My dad was a zoo veterinarian so there were animals and animal things all over. It's funny the things a memory retains. At one end of the living room was a TV of the era, some heavy thing with fake wooden sides. At the other end were my dad's book cases, floor to ceiling, and a big antique chair Mum had bought him for Christmas, which meant we had nowhere to put the Christmas tree any more. I had come into the room, pulled to investigate those giddy whoops, that irresistible attraction of adults behaving like children. And at that volume, really like they should be sent to bed.

I will always remember coming in behind my mother and aunt, with the two of them blocking my view to all else. Music was coming from the TV, and from the two sisters a sort of Bacchic rapture. Mum was wearing tight blue jeans tucked in to white cowboy boots with silver discs on them. She had a perm. Christine, also slim and darkly glamorous to me, who at six was a pudgy blonde tomboy, was spinning Mum under her arm in twirls. They were laughing and gyrating their hips and singing. It made me a bit shy. Truly I had not seen this funny behavior in these two women—both pillars of maternal love and discipline—and in fact I had never seen it in anyone. We are ordered people in England, so they say. Not boogie dancers. But it went on.

"Just. Soooooo gorgeous! So charismatic! Have you ever seen anything like that dancing Linda? I mean it was just so fantastic!" This was Christine, suddenly quite interesting. "Fantastic" was her word for the special only. I remember the exact tone of that long *sooooo*. "I mean I just loved it. That man is so entertaining. Let's watch it again! Right now!"

"Oooh yes! He was rather lovely." This was my own mother, in the '80s, doing something in front of the TV that might be referred to as swooning. The music was still going. I remember that I walked around the back of them to sit beside the fireplace by the rhino, where I could see the TV. I think I was probably acknowledged in passing, but that's not in my memory. What firmly is in my memory, is a crowd of people dancing on the TV set with credits coming up the screen over them. Just lots of people together dancing closely, my mum and aunt cooing, also dancing and happy. Then there was, to a six-year-old, an extremely embarrassing moment I wished I had not been in the room for. On the screen, a man with bushy hair had stopped dancing and kissed a woman, also with bushy hair, right on the lips. Christine's hands were on her heart. Mine were right over my eyes as I looked away. How awkward! When I was three, I would listen to a cassette of fairy tales in the car, and there was a part in *Sleeping Beauty* where Prince Philip kisses Princess Aurora. I'd be so embarrassed that my mum could hear it too, that I would have to either (a) talk loud, (b) be asleep or (c) have a coughing fit. I got to know the tape and I could remember driving down the bumpy lane, wishing we'd get home before that kiss came. The mortification of any physical intimacy in front of a parent starts younger than we might think, and in 1988 this kiss was not only on the TV driving my family into silliness, but they had decided to replay the last fifteen minutes of the film.

I could see the tape rewinding, silver lines over the screen, while I sat down, allowed now to be part of the second screening in my family of the last dance of *Dirty Dancing*. As I reflected from Ithaca, I could clearly remember sitting by the empty fire grate and stroking the mahogany rhinoceros, but I couldn't remember the opening moments of the dance at all. I just had a mental image of the bushy-haired man jumping onto his knees off a stage, dancing with other people, dancing with the lady in the white dress. The music, heard so many times since, *Now I've had the time of my life, and I owe it all to you.* Those things, and the sweaty dancing in unison in between the chairs, the hooded eyes of the male lead, the romantic gaze. This was a world I was not yet part of, with an age still in single digits. As the credits rolled again, I had watched the temporary infatuation of my mum and her sister who joined the show again with their jiving in the sitting room, all the while swearing devotion to this heartthrob dancer whose name they only caught on the second attempt. Patrick Swayze.

"Christine," my mother had declared in seriousness. "I think I am going to marry him." (That wasn't, by the way, what happened after her divorce.)

The second memory of Patrick Swayze was from about seven years later, when I was roughly twelve. Again, not so much Patrick Swayze direct, but what he created in other people. My friend Prue and I lived close and would offer quarterly performances for our families, long-practiced, argued over, and mostly very bad indeed. They were usually dancing, though God knows why and why no-one stopped us: we had both been kicked out of ballet class at school. It was the devilment of parents probably, who would laugh so happily at these shows (I wore a swimming hat in one, attempting to pass off a balding man). We believed they were laughing with us. The late '80s had been about Michael Jackson, of course, and then when I was twelve it was time to become Baby and Johnny, easily cast because I was the short one and Prue's mum had a thing at the time for the "pudding bowl" haircut. Prue had to be the guy. And so, she was my hero.

I think we practiced that last dance in *Dirty Dancing* for maybe a hundred hours. I can still see it, in front of mirrored wardrobes in her long bedroom, me staring at the floral carpet waiting for her to come and tip my chin up and beckon so I could feign love. To this day I can remember how the feet go in the opening fifteen seconds, like muscle memory, and I can remember Prue's mum screaming up the stairs in anger, "What the hell was that, Prue?" after I jumped off her bed to get lifted but instead landed with a floor-shaking thud. I can't remember performing the finished version of this Dance, which I now appreciate, and I have absolutely no recollection of watching the movie to learn the Dance, or even of watching Patrick Swayze with Jennifer Grey. I just remember the hours and hours practicing, focused and laughing, in pursuit of something we'd never have. We were hopeless. But we were committed anyway to the magic of *Dirty Dancing*.

Then there was a very long gap in my memory, where I could recall no thought of him. In my life, in my entire generation, the actor to swoon over was Brad Pitt. Johnny Depp was the choice if you were trying to be edgy, but as I argued it you really meant Brad Pitt and his perfect face. For me, the actors not to miss were the older classics, still wheeled out since they hadn't yet found a new one: Jack Nicholson, Al Pacino and Ian McKellen; Judi Dench, Meryl Streep and Angelica Houston among the women. I liked a few new actors. Carey Mulligan, Anne Hathaway, Ryan Gosling. But Patrick Swayze wasn't on the list. He hadn't featured and failed with me, I just couldn't remember him. I didn't know how many movies he had made—whether there were just a few or lots of them, or why I couldn't remember seeing many more. Obviously, I was aware of who he is, but in England I didn't remember him having any big press attention. Maybe I was too young (I was born in 1981), or just didn't follow the media enough. When *Ghost* made it, I was maybe nine or ten. That was the only other Patrick Swayze movie I could think of.

So truly, my third memory of Patrick had been last night in Ithaca. Seventeen years after the Dance show with Prue, when I was twenty-nine and a few months.

I was awake early, thinking about it. Like the night before, I had a hundred questions I wanted answering immediately. Was this real? Why him? Why was he there? What was going to happen? Was I stupid to even contemplate believing it? But really, while I fought myself not to acknowledged it, I felt a little bit embarrassed. *Patrick Swayze. The movie star.* Where had he been while I had been asleep? Was he watching me? Now? It didn't matter that I was never a big fan. I never disliked him, I was just never a follower. But he was still a famous movie star, still that handsome, charismatic dancer I of course remembered, and the thought of him walking around this terrible little flat telling me what to do in a seemingly self-assured tone made me feel self-conscious, bad at writing, going nowhere, and probably a little bit fat. I know I wasn't happy about those ten extra pounds, which to a dancer's eye probably looked like twenty-five.

I wasn't quite sure how to act or arrange myself if I got up. I was not quite sure, actually, of who I was at all. I wasn't sure if it was right for him of all people to just turn up in the middle of my summer class in literary theory. But I realized that I believed it. My sense of reason told me it was too unreasonable to think the universe has just fabricate a false experience around me. But why? My eternal, damning, overused question word. Always why.

I thought of everything I could about Patrick Swayze. I really concentrated and pushed my brain round corners. I knew of course about the two movies. I could see myself watching *Ghost* with my dad in the cinema on his Sunday of the month. Yes, I must have been ten, terrified of the big black groaning blobs that drag bad people away.

I knew that he was a dancer people loved. Patrick Swayze is pretty much synonymous with the word "dancing". I knew he was big in the 80s: my mental image of him was with that mullet hair. And I was sure then, when I really tried to remember all references, that I had seen him several months ago on the big rack of magazines in Stanford's gym, front page. I vaguely remember wincing at an image of him clearly suffering, looking gaunt in a hat, next to some garish byline, possibly in yellow. I was forcing my memory now, maybe making up the yellow color. Perhaps the font had been green. I remembered choosing not to pick up the magazine, and the feeling of distaste. I just did not want to see Patrick Swayze suffering in a magazine. Or anyone suffering in a magazine for that matter. It felt wrong. That's all I knew about him. That, and the realization he obviously had since died, had lived a life and died without me knowing anything about it. It was a strange thought. He had died, which I felt sad for, and then somehow he had come to Ithaca, told me to write, and said *See ya*.

What on Earth had I got to do with him?

Nothing, I thought. I didn't even know if he had a partner, I realized, or the several successive wives Hollywood heroes seem to have. I didn't know if he had children or where he lived or how old he was. Even when he died or what from. I still could think of absolutely no connection between us: no interest either way. But I had felt that abstract closeness of him in my living space. And the question was under my skin now. *What was he doing there?*

My best friend called me the next day. "Guess what! The first song on my radio this morning was *Unchained Melody*! A sign!"

"Maybe," I said, happy for her light heart about the whole situation.

"Take on a spirit guide here if you've got a chance! Get out of the box. Academia is boring!"

We watched *Dirty Dancing* that night together, over Skype, each of us on our separate TVs. We had to stop and start twice to get the dialogue in unison.

Afterwards, we talked a bit about the movie, which had been set at the fictional resort Kellermans, in the Catskill Mountains and not far from where I was. We laughed about the off-putting the character of the resort owner's son. He had been the other love interest for Baby Houseman, and a total creep. I said to her, "I think God must love me if He is out there. Because I think if God didn't love me, he would probably not have sent me Johnny Castle, but Mr. Kellerman's son."

CHAPTER SEVEN

A few days later, I had been to class and then had been for lunch with my new friends. The afternoons were usually for private reading, and I had started splitting my afternoon time between reading Derrida and picking up the pendulum. Sometimes, I spent a few hours trying to do some creative writing, but mostly found myself writing personal essays rather than fiction. I spent a long afternoon with the essay I had written about Nonny just before she died. In it, I had tried to capture the bittersweet nature of visiting a nursing home, knowing that life was coming to a close for those people, and yet many still had so much life in their memoires. I had sat with a latte and had edited bits of it, thinking about her.

He was there when I walked in the door in the early evening. I could feel the presence now.

R-E-A-D-I-T.

"What, now?" My pendulum swung to *yes*. "Out loud?" Another swing. *Yes*.

Shit! Patrick Swayze wanted me to read my personal essay out loud to him. Now.

"This is Patrick?" I asked.

It swung *yes*.

I pulled up Finder on my laptop and looked for the essay I had been revising that afternoon. *Where was he? Behind me?*

I opened the file and glanced over it with my pendulum still in hand. The pendulum started moving. In this slow but still amazing form of communication he told me he didn't like the title.

"*The Departure Lounge*? Really? Why not?"

T-O-O-I-R-O-N-I-C-T-O-O-D-A-R-K.

I had liked the title. I felt a bit deflated that he didn't. What if he also didn't like any of the thirty-two double spaced pages that followed?

R-E-A-D.

So, I did. It was getting close to dusk in Ithaca and there was a candle in a glass jar shining to the side of me. With the sunlight fading, the only other light in the room was a lamp in the hallway and the brightness of my laptop. I felt like I was on a stage, alone in a vast cavernous space in front of a professional judge.

I looked at the document, and just quietly started to read aloud. At first, I was unsure of my voice, whether I should just read this flat or lend it some character. He had given no direction. The essay started in Nonny's voice as she had introduced me around the nursing home a year or so before. It began with her saying, loudly, "And this . . . is Barbara."

I felt awkward to perform it with the same old lady voice I could remember her speaking with. I felt silly trying to highlight the humour I wanted my listener to find. I kept reading, and when the funny lines came out into the thick air around me, I wished I could gauge my audience as he was gauging me. *Where was he?*

I kept reading. Of course, I want him to feel what I had done. I wanted him, since he had demanded I read the essay, to give a thought to this old lady I had been writing about, who had the love affair of her life during the Second World War, and who had fled it for security and for the appearance of doing "the right thing". I wanted him to feel the same poignancy I had felt when a man had once stood up in the dining room in that nursing home in England having lost his wife that morning. He had taken his wife's photograph to every person to hold, talking about what it took to make a man feel cracked.

I found as I read aloud in this close space, that I wanted him to care. I didn't know him from Adam. But this was part of my heart. Perhaps he had even seen Nonny on the other side. Imagine that. I missed her and wanted to validate her relatively small life compared to his, a seamstress turned grandma who had made it to her nineties. I wanted him to laugh with me and with her, not at her when I read out the sweet things about aging that had made me chuckle. She had a crossword with the clue "well-known phrase for feeling of joy: ------- pink (7)". She had responded to it by drawing extra boxes off the side of the grid, and then writing 'champagne'. I wanted him to know that the hard and fast rules were not her thing, not in life when she dared say no to a loveless marriage, not in that nursing home when she'd do the crossword as she damn well pleased. She lived the spirit of the good rules of the life, not the letter of them. It was important to me, that she received some testimony. I stopped reading, without expecting it.

"You know, she just did it her way," I said to the air quietly. I had let the pendulum drop. I kept reading. I read about the moments in our lives when she told me about her affair with this American soldier who begged for her to leave with him but she couldn't. I kept going through flashbacks and flash-forwards. I read through the time at age ninety-two when she and my mum and Christine drank a liter of Baileys in three hours, which was so rare for her. She was so sweetly merry and hysterically laughing in her hands when I came home that I cried with laughter not knowing her punch line. I let him hear the time I'd guessed I would never see her again with the pendulum's prediction of her death date looming. I read about the time I interviewed her in the home about her life, and her ninety years of the ups and downs of an average life. I had interviewed so that she might be captured, because even if the world had not recognized her, to me she had been so special.

I shared the answers from the interview and the shattering of my heart as I left the nursing home that day, with the view of an old lady in a flimsy white nightgown with orange flowers turning back down the hall to her room. I hadn't seen her again.

I said it all to an empty room that was saturated

with sensation and emotion.

"It's so funny," I said when I stopped again, presuming he was still listening, "to think she has found her way to me in Ithaca. I would never have had a clue if she hadn't once owned a pendulum. Isn't it weird? Just those little things seem to set parts of your life up." I wondered fleetingly what the equivalent little things in his life had been.

The pendulum was on the table beside me, lying on top of the letter G. I finished the story. There were three photographs of her at the end, which had been well-chosen by my mother when I'd been asked to submit this essay at Stanford. She was ninety-three in the first, then forty-four, then eighteen. "I don't know if you can see them, but that's what she looked like." I left the images on my screen and got up to get a glass of water.

I left for a few minutes. I went to the bathroom, poured another glass of water, and then I picked up the moonstone again. It was still for a few seconds, and then decisively it spelled out just nine letters before it was still again.

K-E-E-P-G-O-I-N-G.

I put the pendulum down and made dinner.

I could feel his presence while I was cooking simple Thai food. It was peaceful and still. I knew that I was definitely not alone, but I didn't feel like he was particularly trying to talk either. I wasn't sure whether I should sit and work more on my essay about Nonny or read for my course, or something else. I felt sad. I was aware that I carried a ball of sadness in my torso. I wandered round the apartment for a few minutes, looking for mindless jobs. Edward would be out with his guy friends this evening. In the end, I sat down and pulled out my moonstone. I let it roll in my hands.

I knew there was a spirit there. I knew now that there was an afterlife. That much I was accepting. But a nasty thought kept creeping into my mind. *How did I know this was really him?* This presence could be anyone. A pretender. Just some dude who died in Ithaca who knew of a famous man. I felt sad when I reflected on my grandmother. I felt very vulnerable, and perhaps more vulnerable I had felt ever before, especially with not knowing my personal direction and with this spirit around asking me to trust him that he was really Patrick Swayze.

I wanted it to be true, because if not, someone was really being crappy to me, on a huge scale. I wanted it not to him too, because the implications of being associated with him were scary to me. Obviously, more people than me would need to know, or deserve to know. He wouldn't be there for just me; that would make no sense. He would ask me to tell people. I don't think I can describe just how exposed and defenseless that thought made me feel when my life was lacking in solid ground.

But I knew I could not just avoid this

circumstance in my life. The circumstance felt like a baby left in a crib on the doorstep, or how it might feel to stumble across important evidence at a scene of a crime. It felt like those scenarios in the sense that it had crossed my path and whatever my personal worries or situation, it would be wrong to ignore it. It also felt like the abandoned baby or the crime scene evidence because I was cautious about getting involved. It might mean questions and attention I wasn't particularly sure I could handle.

I picked up my journal and my pendulum and started quietly asking questions aloud. My mood was flat, and I pulled them from nowhere planned.

"Did you have many wives?" I asked.

The moonstone didn't go forward or back but swung in a big circle, high in energy. I hadn't seen that. "What does that mean?"

I got the word *funny*. Then as I was looking confused, it swung again in a circle, then changed in a second to the left and right of a very clear *no*.

I thought I got the point and smiled. I had been called out on a Hollywood stereotype. Who in the film business just has one spouse? Him, obviously. "How long were you married?"

"Longer than you've been here." That felt like a long time. I built up the courage to ask.

"Were you happy?"

"Yes. Mostly."

"Good." I wasn't sure what to say. "What exactly

do you want me to write?"

"Mediumship, friendship, and love."

"Why?"

"You can. You can make the world a better place with your pen."

I had heard that since I was at school. It was amazing to now hear it from him.

"What does it mean to you that I do that? Write I mean?" I was trying to figure out why this might really be Patrick Swayze.

"Everything," he said, then repeated it. E-V-E-R-Y-T-H-I-N-G.

I was quiet.

The pendulum moved without a question.

"We got married," he spelled.

"When?"

"Second time."

"Huh?"

"On a horse."

"You married the same woman twice?"

"You would have." I felt the smile and warm heart.

That was cute of him. I smiled too.

"Did you divorce her and then got married again?"

A swing to *no*.

"Just for love?" I asked.

"I guess."

Again, I felt a smile behind me.

Please, I thought, *don't be a pretender. I know the world is full of crazies. Let there be a world full of real and true people too.*

"Did you have any children?" I asked.

No.

I just asked it, intrusive or not. "Why not?"

"Problems." Then I wished I hadn't asked that.

"Did you regret that? No children?"

Edward and I had started to discuss children. Our reticence on the subject had made me quietly wonder if our match was quite right. We were avoiding trying.

Yes. So, for Patrick there perhaps had been some hardship with trying for children. It was only a swing forward and back, but somehow I could feel and interpret emotional energy in the air the more I was focused. There were no eyes to read yet.

It had been a long day and a long evening. I felt fatigued. This was becoming personal, and heartfelt. This spirit and I had lived some similar emotional terrain, I could tell.

I still didn't feel I had proven to myself who he was. I had to.

CHAPTER EIGHT

The next day, I resolved after class to get somewhere. I was prepared to sacrifice my reading for the afternoon. I just needed some certainty. I needed it about him and I needed it about mediumship in my life. I still didn't class what I was experiencing as mediumship, but I was becoming more sensitive to presence again. I could feel the emotional communication more after several hours of having him around. I didn't know if I'd get my answers in a day, but I was ready to address all those calls I had had to the spirit world, and either face it or walk away.

I was still with the moonstone. I was getting frustrated with the laboriousness of it, but wasn't developed enough to work without it just yet.

In the kitchen, I stated my case. He was there, as gently persistent as I was. "I know there is no real reason for a random spirit to claim your life and name, Patrick," I said. It was the first time I had used the name to address him. "But this is still very strange. You have nothing to do with me and I am in Ithaca. I thought you were a California person. I am going to ask you some questions. I have to."

The pendulum was still. I had cut into an easy atmosphere by building a wall. I could feel it in the room between us.

"Did you have animals?" I asked.

"Tons." It felt to me like I'd just asked him the most boring question on the earth, apart from his favourite colour, but as a vet's daughter and an animal woman, it said something to me when someone was an animal person.

Perhaps he was waiting to be asked all the dumb questions now. The pendulum was still, giving nothing. I could just sense vibration around me. Energy moving. It wasn't quite a mood but it almost is. Screw it. He might see the irony. I had not prepared my interview.

"What's your favourite colour?"

"Blue." Of course. There was a pause. "Brilliant blues. Teals and happy shades."

"What did you die of?"

"Pancreatic." I noted it.

"When?"

"September." There are no numbers on my letter circle for him to give me a date.

"What is your mum called?"

"Patsy."

"Is she alive?"

"Yeah."

"My dog was Boswell. An Irish Wolfhound. We had tons of cats and that massive dog."

"Well you haven't got one now."

"How do you know?" I asked.

"I'm around."

"Oh." I carried on. I was scribbling all the trivia

down. "What was your dog called?"

The pendulum swung in a circle wing again. Apparently, this was funny, or entertaining. "Cody."

I was trying think of something else to ask. Actually, I could think of loads of things.

"Name a food you like. Liked."

"Why?"

"I want to see what you say."

"Why?" he asked again. I didn't say anything. "Sushi."

"Ok, thanks," I said. Sushi. I was expecting steak. I hated sushi. "Where did you live?"

"When?"

I rolled my eyes. "Whenever!"

"New Mexico."

"Ok." This had taken some time. "Thanks," I said. "I need half an hour." I was really trying to stay all business formality until I felt safe.

I put the pendulum down and stood up. I went to the desk in the fall, opened my laptop and googled Patrick Swayze. I googled "Patrick Swayze home". It told me he had a ranch in L.A. called Rancho Bizarro. I paused on the name. Bizarro.

Los Angeles is not in New Mexico. I was not happy. I googled "Patrick Swayze death" and it said his dates were August 18, 1952 to September 14, 2009. Anyone could know that.

I tried "Patrick Swayze sushi", which gave me my first and I hoped last life experience of starting to feel like a stalker. The internet told me in a few minutes that he loved the food. Could anyone know that? Anyone dead? Maybe I was getting paranoid.

I continued. I entered "Patsy Swayze" and yes, she was his mother. That caught me in my throat. You could see the resemblance clearly in a black and white photo from her youth. She was a choreographer and dance instructor. Same face structure. I kept reading about her. She was now in her early eighties and survived him. A mother who had lost a son. I felt for her. Then I found some good information and ran back into the kitchen to find my pendulum.

"What's her real name?"

H-A-A-P-A-N-I-E-M-I

"What? No! Patsy's real name. Your mother!"

Y-V-O-N-N-E. H-A-P-P-Y-Y-E-T. I felt the tone of the question mark.

"Nope." I ran back to my computer. Yvonne Helen Swayze. Haapaniemi was not in fact a random mess of letters with a mad pendulum but the full maiden name of Lisa Swayze, Patrick's wife. I felt somewhat placated.

I wanted to say something, but I didn't. Patrick's home hadn't been right, and I was still grasping at that possibility. There was still a chance this might not be real. I typed in "Patrick Swayze New Mexico" and in under a second I was faced with a full screen of him in a cowboy hat with his arm round a striking blonde woman with fair skin and a pretty smile. She had her arm round a dog, not called Cody. There was a lake behind them, and trees. I thought she must be Lisa. Patrick himself looked older and thinner than any mental image of him I had. He was grinning under a huge black hat that looked like an upturned plant pot. Lisa had patterns on her lapels and jacket. They went well together, cowboy and cowgirl. I looked further and found the picture was taken in New Mexico the previous year, at their other ranch. The one not in Los Angeles. I was mellowing.

Half-heartedly now, feeling almost cruel for it, I googled "Patrick Swayze Cody". The first two lines of text at the top of the list of links referred to his loss of an eleven-year-old dog called Cody, "my best friend." I caved.

"This cannot be happening to me," I said. "It is just too odd."

I took a few minutes pacing around the apartment without the pendulum. I could feel him following me, but not too closely. I didn't have visual or auditory confirmation, but I had to admit that the information was good.

"You know what I want to know?" I asked. "What on earth are you doing here?" I looked up and over my shoulder as I said it. I was not sure of the etiquette of this spirit guide business. I was not sure he was either. "Will you tell me why you are suddenly claiming to be my guide?"

I realized I would have to sit down again with my

pendulum.

"I chose it."

"Why?" I asked

"I needed you."

"You? Needed me? Why?"

"Because." I was waiting for his responses letter by letter and all he gave me was "because".

"Because?"

"You're not ready to know." "You're" was U R.

"Is that serious? I'm not ready? Why the hell are you here then?" My tone had changed to the negative.

"Because I need you," he said.

"To do what?" I was getting annoyed. I don't tolerate confusion all that well, in case that isn't already clear.

"Tell Lisa."

"Tell her what?"

"That I am real."

Something rose in me that was pure fire. It was totally unexpected but forceful, a defense of myself. "Are you crazy? What do you want me to do, Patrick Swayze? Just call your sweet wife up out of the blue and tell her 'Hello, you have never heard of me, but your late husband has asked me to call you? I'm not even a medium but there you go, please believe me and let me go back to school.' Are you totally insane, Patrick? No! No." For good measure, I added, "No."

The pendulum swung around. Part of the fire was because I wish I could just do it for him, and let God alone know why I had to be the messenger. "Can't you just find a medium?" I asked.

S-U-R-E. Now I felt angry. And probably proud.

"What else do you want?" I asked.

N-E-V-E-R-M-I-N-D.

I felt trapped. This was not fair. I put the pendulum down and made tea. I made a few phone calls to people, not really listening to the small talk and not mentioning anything about the last couple of hours of my life. I was annoyed. But the presence was still there when I had hung up and calmed down a bit. Eventually, I felt softer and I pick the pendulum up again. "I don't know what to do," I said.

"You're not ready to know why I need you because you won't accept it."

"Accept what?" I said, ready to be annoyed again.

"That you are a medium." I really could feel frustration in the air around me. Perhaps I should say in the spirit around me. It didn't feel fair any more to refer to him as air.

"This isn't exactly mediumship," I said. I still had the pendulum. Mediums don't use tools to aid them.

T-R-Y.

"I don't know how!" I was surprised how much I dropped my reserve. I was doing nothing to hide my emotion.

"Forget it. I'll ask you a few questions. Did you have animals?"

"Tons," I said. The pendulum didn't move. We

were still, but I realized he was trying. "I had five cats growing up," I continued, "and a huge dog, and there were parrots and other animals in the house." There was no movement. "I don't know what to tell you. My favorite cat was called Wilhelmina Prudence Velvet Cat. I had another cat called Tottie who wrote a newsletter to the family. I edited and distributed. Oh, okay, I wrote it. She had a big character, always seeming to want to say something. I had another cat that got hit by a car and a favourite that was mauled to death by a greyhound. I love animals, miss cats and I can't have any where I live in California. You've clearly seen." There was still no response. I felt like such an idiot. "We once had a tiger cub in the house, and a bear cub at the same time."

H-O-R-S-E-S-H-I-T.

I laughed. Increasingly I noticed that I could feel the tone of the words coming over and through my mind. With the aid of the pendulum, some sensation was breaking through my mind. I couldn't quite hear, but I knew the words as they were being formed over the bicycle wheel of letters. I knew the tone. The tone of *horse shit* was amused and incredulous. There was a real sense he was attentively listening. It warmed me.

"It's true. We had a giant tortoise for a while which I adored, and then the tiger and bear. My dad had his surgery in the basement of our family home. I'd go down after school to watch him operate. If the patients were well enough they were allowed upstairs. I spent most weekends with him inspecting circuses and looking at bigger animals."

'Like horses?" I got the word horses just from the letter H. I could feel the word coming through me rather than hear it, and I knew it was right. It was confirmed when I got the remaining letters of the word. I was willing to concentrate. I didn't state that I was becoming more attentive, I just really gave my attention and effort.

"No horses. The nearest is a zebra. They were all exotic zoo animals."

"I had horses. Loved them. You should read about that online too."

"Ha, ha. I believe you."

"My questions," he said.

"Okay."

"Did you ever ride a horse?"

"When I was younger I rode with my friend Prue. I had a little grey one called Sparky from the riding school and she had a huge one called Big Lady who chucked her off over a jump and terrified us both. It didn't last much after that."

"You need to get back on." There was almost a sound in the air around me. A vowel sound in the word on. I was scared I was imagining it. I wanted to keep the conversation going to try to hear.

"It took me a while. I only got back on last year on the beach at Half Moon Bay in California. I loved it. I guess I'm once bitten twice shy."

"That's a real shame."

"Perhaps you're good at what I'm bad at. I ran away from ballet after two terms. I ran away from horses after watching a bad fall, and I even ran away from acting when I got to Cambridge."

W-H-O-A.

I was sure I had heard it at the same time it had come across the pendulum. My heart was beating. I didn't want to tell him unless I messed something up. I let him keep asking questions.

"I didn't know you had been to Cambridge. Smart cookie."

"Sometimes," I said.

"Why no ballet?"

I laughed. "Have you seen my thighs? I did one school concert and the tape shows Prue and I watching the other dancers and repeating their steps three seconds behind."

"That's my kind of show."

How diplomatic. Somehow I doubted it. I had noted his mother and wife were as proficient in ballet and dance as he was. But I appreciated his grace.

"Can I say something?" I said. "I think I can feel what you are saying before you spell it. Can you do something? Just give the first letters of each word? I think I am starting to intuit them."

O-C.

Of course! I could feel it. It wasn't quite hearing. "You said of course. Say something else!" Suddenly, I was all command.

D-Y-H

"Do you have siblings? Is that what you said?" I asked, excitedly. "Are you saying these things aloud as it comes on the pendulum or just thinking it?"

It swung back and forward *yes*.

"I have a half-sister, twelve years younger, who is my dad's daughter. I'm my mum's only child and grew up just with her. Sorry, is it aloud or thought, what you've been saying?"

"Aloud." The pendulum just gave me an *A*.

"Wow." I said. "I wonder how all this works."

"Me too." I was grasping the words as they came, and was trying with my eyes closed. "I didn't study it much, but I want you to keep going."

"Ok. Wow it's like opening my brain differently. Or reopening it."

"Do they know you're a medium?"

"No."

"How come?"

It was the first time someone had asked me straight out about this gift I had in acceptance of it rather than in defiance of it. I sat still with the question and gave the answer from my heart. It was an answer that came from deep within, long forgotten. "I walked away from talking to spirits to be accepted rather than abandoned."

"Jodie, I need a minute." I wasn't quite picking up a voice, but I knew there was a presence of a voice. It was vibrating around me.

I got up and put the kettle on for tea. Had I said something wrong?

"Oda Mae felt that experience, I think." I hadn't quite heard that sentence, but I had the impression of it. Whoopi Goldberg in a pink suit flashed through my mind briefly as I stood at the stove.

I ran back to the table, noting everything, and returning to the safety net of the pendulum.

"I think she felt the rejection too," he said. Oda Mae was the character Whoopi Goldberg had played in one of the films Patrick had starred in. She had played a reluctant medium. "I am starting to understand the movie more. I can't help but think of it."

"I saw *Ghost* a long time ago," I said. "I was with my dad."

"One of a ton of movies I made. The only one on this theme. A long time ago. Did you like it?"

"No!"

I actually felt the whole energy of the room drop by one octave. Like I had sunk the floorboards.

"Sorry!" I said. "I mean, yes I know it is a brilliant, outstanding movie, but I was ten and it had scary characters and the end made me cry. I didn't like crying in front of my dad."

"Me either."

"It's a great movie. I'll watch it again. I like Whoopi. Did you?" I asked.

"God, yes." He said it as though he had actually said it to God. I could feel the heart of what he was saying. It was easier to feel the emotions from Patrick than to "hear" the words. "She made a good movie a great movie."

I smiled at the life he had lived. I didn't have many details, but I was pleased he had walked with special people. It might have been one part among a long list of very different roles (my earlier googling had shown a long list of about thirty movies on his Wikipedia page), but I was pleased he had been a medium's friend on a screen, even if she was fictional. It made me feel a bit safer to think I might have his empathy where I had not, as a younger person, had much empathy with this subject of seeing ghosts.

CHAPTER NINE

Over lunch the next day, I sat with my laptop in a café on Cornell's campus and did some more leisurely googling of Patrick Swayze. I found an article whose byline was a quote from him. "New Mexico is my healing place." The article was from September 14, 2009. In fifty seconds, I learned that I liked him. I had already started to like him from our conversation the day before, but I learned as I read that I would have liked Patrick as a man. I saw the connection between what I was reading on the screen and the persona that had been around me for several days now. Or perhaps for longer.

The article was a brief obituary, which detailed his career and relationship in a few lines. It had quotes from him in the 1980s at the height of his fame, up until he had spoken in 2009 on his battle with pancreatic cancer. Every quote endeared me to him in its own way. There was blackness in his humor, and I got the sense of someone who was at once shy and unashamed. His quotes suggested he also had the sort of vulnerability that a man can hold yet somehow still qualify for Marlboro man masculinity. He was not fluffy. Not floral. Not a *luvvie*, as we used to call actor types in the Footlights drama group when I did my undergraduate degree. He seemed to talk straight.

Together, these quotes—the first words of his I

had ever read—gave some solidity to my own first impressions. I was grateful for it. When you're dying of cancer, he had been asked, what do you do? "You go to work." I had felt some of that no-nonsense work ethic forced at me this week, with his will that I write and keep going. He was quoted in an article on the topic of "looking for curveballs" in his life, and the "ancient energy. . . ancient spirits and spirituality" that he could sense at his land at New Mexico. He had sure given me a spiritual curve ball. It seemed that the character (or the soul) mostly stays the same after we've passed over.

Patrick had talked once, the article continued, of being "fed up with that Hollywood blockbuster mentality". As a result, he had made some of his atypical film choices. I liked that. It would be hard not to. Then I learned he played a drag queen, which surprised me. I liked that fact too. It made me smile to myself. I liked the daring and the range. I liked the implied spirit behind the work.

Patrick was quoted on the loneliness and boredom of fame, and how much of a hoax it might have been. This was a little clichéd for me, too much the same story you hear pretty much every time you're faced with a celebrity interview in the wait to see the doctor. It's just so hard, being world renowned for what you love, and that old press release. I didn't feel a lot of sympathy for that expression. To denounce the privilege of fame felt ungrateful, or unaware of how people without privilege live. It felt ungrateful for his own talents and their rewards.

Perhaps it had been one off-hand comment, but I was looking for my own real impressions and opinions of him without his presence around. It didn't matter to me that he had been a big star, or that his presence in my summer apartment had intimidated me somewhat. He was asking something of me and I wanted to know if I really liked him or if he were just persuading me to. I was being real with him and wanted to know he was real.

The series of quotes in his obituary told me that he seemed honest, and blunt, and perhaps a little kooky. Whatever his opinion on fame, which admittedly I had never lived, the other qualities were all winners with me.

I read more about his self-professed "wild-man edge" that lead to "sabotage" and regret, and his thirst for exploration over wasted time. In all of these little soundbites, I started to sense a character who might legitimately find himself here, trying to talk to a possible medium in Ithaca. It just about felt psychologically real.

He had spoken of determination, of having to "fight his way up", and of the preciousness of hope. Both those comments rang true. He had suffered, I learned, in many ways. He had learned cynicism. But when I read of his opinion of *Dirty Dancing* as a movie about "when you just need to love somebody with all your heart and be loved back", I wondered if cynicism had been a convenient persona. I thought there was a romantic under that façade, and a dreamer, and someone who hoped. Someone who wanted to bring joy to the world. I used every faculty I had to understand emotionally and spiritually, as well as intellectually, what he might be doing in trying to persuade me to recognize mediumship. I was somewhat stressed by his claim of needing me, but I read so that I could try to be sensitive to him.

I continued with a few more articles. I liked that his life was full, that he seemed committed to his creativity and to some self-understanding, and I liked the spontaneous, lack of bubblegum self you rarely seemed to get in an industry of manufactured stardom and all its red-tape PR. The sense that he was always searching and never quite found himself was there in the subtext. As was a man who needed his space, like I do, who was a wildlife conservationist, like my dad is, who was real animal person, like both my dad and I, and who was likely impassioned about something—be it good, bad, ridiculous, who cares—all of the time, without rest. If that happy passion is there I can forgive someone almost anything.

One journalist wrote that his career was about making cult films, which to me was very different from blockbusters. The word caught me: I had written and taught at Stanford about cult fiction, and just what that might be. Cult is a bit edgier than mainstream. It has a different way of viewing the world. It was interesting to think about his life choices as he was asking me to ponder mine.

I wondered what Patrick knew about me already. I wondered what it was he thought I wasn't ready to know.

I didn't pick up the pendulum that night. I needed some mental rest and went out with Mike, Paul and a woman called Ariana. We drank martinis and a bottle of wine together, talking about the course and the different places on the Earth that we'd come from. None of us mentioned much about our hobbies or activities outside of school. We were just getting to know one another. So, I didn't feel the need yet to mention the pendulum. I was grateful for the mental rest, and after some easy fun with them I slept well and woke up the next day feeling rested and ready to contribute in class.

I had not yet mentioned my new experiences to Edward or anyone else in our small close-knit group back in California. I had had a few emails from them all, but email didn't seem the right format. Edward was spending lots of time with two couples we were close to. They had promised to take him under their wings and not leave him home alone for six weeks. I wasn't quite sure what my husband's reaction would be. I knew it would likely be cautious but open to listening. But one of the couples he was with, although they were my good friends, would be totally closed on the topic of an afterlife. I didn't want to call him and talk about it only for him to then share it with this couple face-to-face and not be there to defend myself. I had drowned my sensitivity to the other side once already. Now it seemed to be coming back, it still felt too precious and fragile to talk about widely. So far, only my mother and my best friend knew, and that was enough for me. I didn't like to keep a secret, but at the same time, I had come to Cornell to find my next step, academic or otherwise.

The next evening, I was cooking at home in the small kitchen space. I was making an Italian dish, and was splashing tinned tomatoes into a pan. I was alone and absent-minded, pulling warming tomatoes apart with a wooden spoon, thinking I should have turned the heat down on the onions. They had browned at the edges. There was a bottle of red wine open on the work surface beside me, opened for cooking but now missing its first half glass, which was about to turn into a second half glass. It was a Rioja, one of my favorites. I had found it in a little grocery store on the edge of town. I still bought Spanish and European wines despite living in California, which insulted lots of people.

There was music playing from the hallway, piano covers of Radiohead songs. I love the piano, and listened to piano music when I was relaxing as much as Edward could bear. His preference was a much faster beat, often electronic. Heart-bashing rather than heart-opening, I used to tell him, perhaps a bit critically. For me, the beat of his fast techno music felt like a repeated punch in the chest. I preferred the more subtly stirring effect of natural sound.

I chopped a salad, laid the table for myself, and searched through the cupboards to find oregano. The engineering student actually had a pretty well stocked spice cupboard.

My pan was hissing, still too hot. I always got it almost just right, cooking, but with one notable thing wrong. Like the time the I made a killer risotto and set the pan on fire. Or the complicated Thai curry with the orange juice. But pasta is my forte, my safety net, any style.

I crushed some more garlic, always more garlic, and dropped it into the pan. I looked down at my plum tomatoes, doing nicely, and considered pepper. At my right ear, there was a touch of nothing. I twitched. I kept stirring, and flicked at my ear without much notice, like a cat might. I went at the tomatoes again with my spoon. They were softening. There was another twitch at my side. Then it came.

"That aint the right recipe." I froze. Dropped the spoon. "You gotta put another can in."

I am English English. Patrick's vowels took forever. The Ts were Ds. *Godda.* The 'a' sound wasn't the clipped British 'can'. It was *ca-an.* Soft but too long. The word 'in' had been spoken like it had another syllable. Rolling. Not 'in' to my ear, but *eeyun*.

My spine could feel that missing "can". My soul reached to the heavens and into the earth again in gratitude of it. He had spoken. He was next to me. The voice had been radio-perfect. As I am alive, that was his voice. Undeniable.

"Patrick!" I shrieked, spinning around. "Patrick, I heard you! My God, you sound so Southern! Did you really speak that drawl?"

It hadn't been some revelatory moment. It hadn't been some personal message, or some phrase of simple wisdom that I later learned Patrick is prone to. But truly, I hugged that wrong recipe with its missing tomatoes in my heart and soul. "I can hear you! I can actually really hear you! Not just like impressions on my mind, but the real voice! That Texan voice!" It really was like a gift from God. The gratitude that poured through my heart gave me a perspective on life that has never left me since.

The energy around me changed as though the circus had just come to town. That's the best way I can describe it. There was real heart-opening excitement and activity in the air. Perhaps I had been as much of a miracle to him as he had been to me. I felt a light, feather-like touch at my shoulder.

I spun around and there he was. It was over. The doubt, the nagging, the worry that I had somehow dreamed it or it someone was fooling me. It was over. I was glad there was a glass of wine in my hand. I took a gulp of it.

Standing in front of me, inches from me, with his back to the window, was Patrick Swayze. He was still, and smiling. He looked maybe forty. I just stared at him. It had been more than the second of confirmation I had hoped for. So far, it was maybe six or seven seconds. He didn't appear even to register that I was spellbound, holding a wooden spoon in one hand and a glass of wine in the other, my mouth open, not giving a monkey's eye that more Bolognese sauce was dripping all over the floor. It really, really was him. Really.

It occurred to me that perhaps he hadn't realized I had just seen him.

"I can see you," I bleated.

"What do you mean?"

"Mee-un," I said.

"What?"

"Say another thing."

"Another thing." He smiled.

"Another thee-ung," I said, imitating his accent.

The tomatoes were bubbling over the edge of the pan. I did not care. Not even a shred. Let them pour.

"I think you are a medium."

I didn't know if they did some sort of Heaven Botox or released all the stress of life when you crossed over, or if everyone in Hollywood looked like this, but Patrick was the most stunning sight I had ever seen. Just looking at him somehow gave me a new faith in the world. In the whole cosmos. He looked pure.

"They won't believe me." The words poured out of my mouth before I could even compute them.

"Huh?"

"That I can do this," I said. The words weren't coming from my conscious mind. They were coming from some old wound in my heart.

"Of course they will," he said.

Despite my euphoria, a fear rose in me without regard to my preference. It seemed to take over, masking everything. I couldn't reason it away. My vision of him started to slip, and I literally could not control it.

I stood still, ready to cry. I could feel on the inside that he was talking to me, but I was trapped inside an inner shell again and couldn't actually hear the words. I was still standing with the spoon, but I couldn't quite feel myself. I felt calm enough but numb, like a true fear had hit me. I had a few flashbacks as I stood there, and all were of being ridiculed. They were from years ago. I was surprised to find that these dormant memories were still affecting my consciousness, and thus my everyday experience of the world.

I sat down and spoke aloud. I explained what was going on. I said that I thought I had heard him because I had committed the intent and effort to it, and that I had been well rested, open, and calm. I was trusting. I was not trying too hard. But I told him I had lost the sight and hearing again, just as quickly as it had come.

I was panicked. But I tried to stay calm. I knew intuitively that I had to sit a minute with myself and take control again. I needed to find calm. From a place of calm and rest I had seen and heard. If I returned to that state, which I hadn't been in for a while because of my Stanford exams, then I knew I'd see and hear again.

I thought I heard Patrick say I should eat dinner. I went back to the kitchen and started to finish making the meal. I tried not to cry or let emotion overtake me. I just sat down and ate, still, breathing evenly, and thinking of nothing much. I forced calm upon myself, almost meditatively. Sure enough, eventually my ability to sense him came back. I saw him again, this time as more of an outline with some transparency. Before, he had been more opaque. He had the same shirt on. White with some thin stripes.

"I was bullied," he said. "It stopped me dancing. The way to combat it is to be yourself. You could be suppressing half of what you are here for because you have been put out or put down."

I was stunned that I could hear him. And yet, truly, it felt natural.

"Thank you," I said.

"No, Jodie. You don't get this. 'Thank you' isn't enough, or what I want from you. You a have a gift. I see now that it has been blackened or put to one side by the opinion of others. Half the world is that way. It creates trauma. I want you to face up to this and I will help you. I will help you to get over this."

"Ok," I said. I was silenced by his generosity.

"I want you to practice, practice, practice until your gifts are natural and second nature. Writing is one of them. Mediumship is another."

"I need to write all this down,' I said.

I couldn't take in a lot more that evening. I was overwhelmed. I made notes and journaled a bit about my responses to what was going on. He sensed my need for a bit of restful space I think. He didn't pressure me to see, listen, hear or anything else.

I left the room after I'd washed the dishes. I turned the music off. I had a shower, picked up a book, got into bed and fell asleep after a few pages.

CHAPTER TEN

I finally called my husband with the intention of telling him what had happened. I saw his face on the laptop screen. He wasn't change averse, but at the same time change took him some time. He had been brought up in the Jewish faith, but had explored other traditions via his wide circle of friends. He had meditated with friends from Eastern religions, and lately spoke more about agnosticism and Buddhism. We didn't talk about faith all that much, and I wasn't one hundred percent sure where he would stand. We didn't have any sort of regular spiritual practice in our lifestyle. Edward was much more interested in politics and art. He had a good heart and a strong intellect and was still searching for himself, as I was. We weren't sure if our future was in California or back in England, and neither were we sure of our career paths. He worked freelance, which was insecure in the economic climate of the time, and I was on a graduate student stipend. Our families were thousands of miles away. We cared deeply for each other, but we were not on secure and established ground in life. We had been married for just over a year, and the proposal may or may not have been rushed because of the need for his extended visa to stay with me. I don't think either of us was totally sure about that. But we were cosy enough together, and mutually supportive.

I asked him a few questions about what was going on in California. Then he asked how the course was going.

"I don't know," I said. "Its focus isn't very literary. But it is reading and talking about readings. Class presentations. The usual. The usual classroom politics." I had told him already about a few of the characters in the class.

"Are you getting anything out of it?" he asked. "Because I'd rather you were at home."

"I know," I said. "I miss home and you. But something fairly incredible has happened and I need to talk to you about it."

"You're not pregnant, are you?" he looked concerned.

"No! Nothing like that. I think I'm a medium."

"What do you mean you're a medium? You're an academic."

I tried not to sigh, but I could sense already how this was going to go. It wasn't his fault. It was how we were. Or it was the differences between us. There wasn't anything at fault in his expression, but I still felt nervous of it. It was very different from the instant warmth and acceptance I'd had from my best friend.

"I had a visit from Nonny."

"Okay."

"It was really her. She told me all sorts of things that Mum knew to be right."

"You've told your Mum?"

"Yes. I had to. I needed to check some of the details with her."

"Okay. How did she take it?"

"Well. She was tearful. Surprised but accepting," I said.

"Okay. I suppose these strange things happen now and again," he responded. "It could be part of grief. She hasn't been gone long."

"I don't think it's that kind of phenomenon. I think I might be a medium. Perhaps she is a part of waking me up to it. I mean, she is the first person who died who I was very close to."

"But you're not a medium. Isn't it something that is passed through families from childhood or something?"

I was trying not to get defensive. I was trying to keep a sense of rising armour out of my tone and off my heart.

"I have had these experiences, with a pendulum. . ."

"A pendulum?" he interrupted. "Like a Ouija board or something? Since when?" He was startled and also getting defensive. I could see it and I didn't know what to do.

"Since I have been here. You know Nonny had a pendulum."

"I don't think I did," he said. His voice was fairly calm and measured, but he wasn't letting me have a lot of talking space in the conversation.

"Listen. I have started to be able to see and hear things. From the afterlife."

"What?" It wouldn't be fair to say he was accusatory. My heart hurt for the care between us and this new contrast that neither of us had prepared for. I loved him. It hurt to see his confusion, and yet without him experiencing it himself, I didn't know if I would be able to get him to my viewpoint. We had never even discussed any firm belief or otherwise in the afterlife. We had nodded to a colloquial sense of "I hope they have gone to peace in Heaven" after a couple of funerals, but in honesty those comments had represented the standards of societal pleasantries rather than any explored or firm spiritual belief in either of us.

"I have started suddenly to hear and see people who have died. Even someone famous." I didn't know if I had the capacity to make this believable. I could just say what had happened and then it would be believed or it wouldn't be. I didn't have the strength to take on changing people's set ways on things. Besides, that would never be my intention.

"Who?" he asked. "Which famous person?"

"Patrick Swayze." I had said it and I let out a breath that released a tightness on my chest.

"Right," he said. "Wow." It was a fairly flat "wow", but not a mean one.

"It's the truth," I said. "Please believe me."

"Well I know you wouldn't make it up," he said.

"But, well, are you well? Are you rested?"

"Yes I am well. I am sort of rested. This apartment is awful and I can hear every passing car and person outside. But I am rested enough not to be insane."

"Okay," he said. He had a handsome, open face and olive eyes.

The last thing I wanted was to fight with him. I also wasn't sure if I wanted to let him any further in yet.

"Can we talk about something else for a while?"

"Sure. Everything is okay here. The plants are thirsty in the heat." I had a balcony full of pot plants that I had been growing for over a year and he knew I loved them. They'd be in full summer bloom. "I have fresh strawberries and tomatoes every day. I am working ten hours a day, and watching movies in the evenings. The apartment is empty without you."

"I'll be home in a few weeks," I said.

"I know. Four of them."

"Let's plan something fun for when I get back. I have to go. Let's talk later on, okay?"

"Yes, okay," he said.

"I love you," I said.

"I love you," he said. "Ta-ra." He hung up.

I skimmed my reading for the rest of the day. I went to class, said the odd thing here and there, and then came home. It was the same the next day. I didn't do much apart from read, talk to my new friends, and walk in the late afternoons. There was a lake on the campus that I walked round a couple of times in the afternoons. I had an increasing friendship with Paul and Mike, and the light-hearted banter from the two of them kept me from worrying too much about weighty feelings. I felt the presence of Patrick a couple of times, but I found I could resist it if my mood was heavy. In fact, I had to keep my heart heavy to prevent myself from really connecting with him. It was probably immature, but I kept it that way for a day or two so I could stew. It was not fair to him at all, but I wasn't in that mindset. I was struggling, and I was doing it on my own.

On the third morning after the call from Edward, I had the same urge to pick up the pendulum. I noticed the pattern this time. I had arrived in Ithaca with a heavy heart, unaware that it was heavy. The urge to the pendulum might have been more conscious had I had a lighter heart and mind. My experiences with Patrick had felt like a happy miracle, and my heart and mind had become so positive and temporarily unburdened by them that I had started to see and hear what people call the higher vibrations of the cosmos.

My upsetting conversation with Edward and my irritation with my class—both annoying to me through no real fault of their own—had lowered my mood, and my energies in general. I let it be that way. That was the stupidity of it.

I picked up the pendulum, almost smiling despite myself. N-O-N-N-Y. I knew it would be. C-H-I-N-U-P.

"I know, Nonny," I said. "I'm being silly."

N-O-T-S-I-L-L-Y. I couldn't hear her but I knew she was there. J-U-S-T-U-N-D-E-R-S-T-R-A-I-N. I wished I could give her a hug. Her presence gave me some perspective to start shifting my mood. L-I-F-E-IS-L-O-N-G. At least it had been for her. L-I-F-E-W-I-L-L-W-O-R-K-I-T-O-U-T. She was right of course. Doom and gloom was not the way to live life. And it also, I had worked out, was not the attitude if you wanted to experience and support the gift of mediumship.

It was raining that humid Ithaca summer rain. I decided to walk around outside in it and get over myself.

I knew Patrick would be there again when I had brightened my outlook, and he was. I could see him fairly clearly the next time I saw him. I wondered if it was two-way, the need to be bright and positive to make contact. I wondered if other mediums would corroborate.

He did not mention anything personal or heavy the next time I saw him and neither did I. He asked about my walk and then calmly shared easy questions and answers about nothing of much import. He asked if I had been doing any writing. I could still hear him.

"No, I haven't," I said.

"Take it easy," he said.

The next day I thought he was around, but I couldn't see him. There was a miracle to this gift, but it wasn't an easy on-and-off switch. I didn't know the right conditions for mediumship, and I evidently wasn't living them with much consistency.

I picked up the pendulum to try to contact him again.

H-I.

I smiled. "Hi."

D-O-N-E-D-O-N-E-D-O-N-E.

"With what?"

T-H-I-S-P-E-N-D-U-L-U-M.

I felt some hope. "I don't know how."

T-I-M-E-T-O-L-E-A-R-N-I-T.

"Okay." I didn't know this man but he was a kind stranger, and his positive strength buoyed me. I didn't feel inwardly lonely because of him. "I'm in."

I needed knowledge. I was a book person, and my mind was struggling because I didn't have formal training, book knowledge or a teacher.

I googled Barnes & Noble and found that the nearest one was a few miles away, past the downtown. I decided to walk it. It would take the rest of the day to get there and back, but the walk would do me good.

Walking is what I always do to clear my mind,

think something through, or wait for inspiration. I walked down the long hill that leads to downtown, took some side roads past the big East Coast houses and hit a main artery road. It was hot, but it felt good to pound the pavements. Time on my own in the open air had always been important to me, ever since growing up an only child in the English countryside. Despite my lack of view, I kept going beside the passing cars, a CVS, traffic lights. I wanted some good space from the apartment, from the new handouts from the professor, from my emails and from my phone. I didn't want to answer to anyone. I just wanted to make some progress.

Finally, I saw a shopping plaza, the American sort with a big discount shoe chain, a sports outlet, a DIY store and a big book shop. I was glad as soon as I opened the door to see maybe half an acre of books on tables, on shelves, and stacked up in piles by the door. Home ground. There had hardly been a scene in my life where there hadn't been books everywhere.

I picked a couple up from the new fiction table. I couldn't help it. I'm a magpie. Their blurbs were familiar. I knew the authors and their work and what to do with it. I felt firmly rooted on that map, instantly noting likely influences. My specialism at Stanford was going to be contemporary literature. It had been at Cambridge and I had worked in contemporary publishing between Cambridge and Stanford for a couple of years.

I read a few opening paragraphs, interpreting, and enjoying myself. My class at Cornell was not specific to literary students. It was for anyone in any humanities subject, and it was heavily philosophical. The readings were not particularly relevant to my specific interest areas, which was the luck of the draw. It was the same for several others in the class, but the point in our cases was to be in the environment of that kind of intellectual rigour and practice the debating, the interpreting, the presenting, and the transferable skills.

I realized I was missing just about everything that felt like my everyday comfort zone. I put a few new books into my basket. *Cloud Atlas* by David Mitchell. A new collection of David Sedaris. That would be funny. Zadie Smith's new book of essays, which I predicted I would take in during one long evening and admire more and more over time. I remembered meeting her briefly during my days at Penguin in London. She had been a new literary heroine at the time. It felt like miles away in time and space.

I didn't usually go to the spiritual shelves in these huge book shops, but after I had browsed the new book tables, I sought out that section.

I felt totally out of my zone and somewhat judgmental. Now that I had a basket full of literature, I was snobby again at shelves on these woo-woo topics. It was so trained in me and so silly that I gave myself an inward kick. These shelves were going to save me.

I still found some of the titles in turn twee or

nauseating or just too weird. This was all very, very new to me. Books on chatting to aliens and love in tea-leaves and shelves of what would become of us in the supposedly fateful year of 2012 left me feeling bemused. I gathered from the titles on 2012, that many people thought we would either drop dead or dematerialize as a collective. Some huge quantum shift was predicted. I sat and flicked through a few titles. I wondered. Who knew? It just all felt a little fearful. I wanted something confident, and assured. Something researched, and yet something friendly. I needed a friend in the pages of a book.

I ended up choosing a fat three-books-in-one volume by Sylvia Browne, an American psychic medium. I had never heard of her but there was fanfare for her all over the cover and she had half a shelf here all to herself. She had the right face for it, all-knowing eyes and don't-mess-with-me certainty.

Of course, when I had dragged myself back along the miles of flat pavement and then up the hill in the evening humidity, Browne's book was the first I picked up. The literary genius had suddenly lost its pull next to this new material. I read a bit from the medium, who started seeing dead people at a young age and talked about the afterlife. I sat cross-legged in my bedroom with the nasty dark curtains hanging off the rod, and I let myself get engrossed for a couple of hours.

The souls of the dead are around us, she wrote,

and are working to help us and humanity in other planes of reality. She talked about her early experiences and about her own guide. I lost my prejudice against her side of the bookstore. It had been learned in academia and was as easily unlearned once I opened myself to reading with a clear heart.

She was confident in her explanations and her descriptions of her experiences. It had been going on for forty years or more for her, and she had done many readings. I googled her and found out I definitely could not afford her. To her, this was just a part of the universe and we needed to observe it because of the benefit it could bring. She had started a research institute around psychic phenomena before I was even born. Clearly, she had quite a following.

It suddenly struck me very hard that Nonny was dead, and yet somehow not dead too. The word *dead* brought me an odd affect, a strangeness that was new and that I could feel—a response to the flesh and blood and bones of it. There were pictures in my mind of what had happened to her between the time I last saw her in an orange-flowered nightgown and this week. I thought of her going through physical death, and then of her body, a body that I had held and that had held me, going through fire. That had been where I wouldn't let my mind go twenty minutes after her funeral, when people were talking to me about my nice black dress as the crematorium engulfed her. I thought of her after that was over. Obviously, she still had some sort of bodily presence without the physical shell. Where had she gone? How had she got there? Who was she with?

Sylvia Browne's work talks of different visitors from the heavens. Some, she said, worked on in spiritual worlds. In places quite different from here. I tried to imagine it and I tried to accept it.

All I found I was sure of, for my own settled mind, was that there really was an after. *Something* happens.

I had scattered Nonny's ashes in a wood of bright bluebells, hands full of dusty ash and the bone fragments that made me teary. One or two handfuls had been thrown over my mum's back garden where Nonny had loved to sunbathe, and the breeze had sent them back to me, into my hair and face. I'd laughed, standing there with the green cardboard box of my grandma in hand. It was one of those moments in life when something just wasn't quite computing, connecting situation to emotions to response. Mum and her sister had shushed me and told me off quietly, saying it wasn't right to laugh at the ash on my cheeks, be it liver or hand or shoulder blade. It was distasteful, now that she'd died, to find humor in what she would have giggled at. As though now she was dead and her body alone was ashes, she would now be somehow dour and disapproving, unable to see the comedy in the sadness.

But she already still existed to us, I realized

looking back, way before she showed up to tell me things like the flowers at her funeral were a little bright. My mum had chosen them and Christine and I had said they weren't quite to her taste. That day throwing ashes we were conscious, each of us, of what she would be thinking of the scene. She had at least lived on in our hearts and thoughts. That she might appear to verify our impressions and even correct our opinions on what she would had thought was beyond what we had ever imagined at the time.

On my bed in Ithaca, with my new ally Sylvia Browne telling me about real characters not just faint whispers, I wondered why we as a society must change people when they die. Why must we make them somber or frightening, or just evaporated into nothingness, to deal with death? Those practices are for us, I thought, not for them.

CHAPTER ELEVEN

I bought another pendulum in a shop I found on the main plaza in downtown Ithaca. Two actually. The shop was the kind to have incense and hippie clothes, the sort I didn't often go into. Instantly I was attracted to it. I hadn't read all of the Browne book—it was hundreds of pages—but so far although it had comforted me and made me feel much less alone, it hadn't explained any techniques of mediumship.

On the top of the counter was a whole basket of pendulums. I asked the assistant if I could try them.

"Sure."

The first one, a deep orange carnelian, barely moved. The second, a soft pink one, started swinging forwards and backwards. *Yes.* I asked aloud but quietly, if this pendulum was for me. It swung the other way. *No.* It was a shame because it was pretty. The assistant was now watching me over his glasses.

"Are you for this man here?" He had caught me, so I had to at least try to be cute. The stone dropped still. I looked at him and shrugged. "Sorry."

Thankfully, he chuckled. "That's rose quartz. I hardly sell any pendulums."

"Oh, I love them! Maybe I need a rose quartz. Do I need a rose quartz?" *Yes*, it swung. "Do you have any?"

"Small pieces." I had a look at them, not really

attracted to any, but making a mental note. The man rummaged around in the basket and pulled out a clear one on the end of a chain. It wasn't a spherical cone-shaped point in shape like many of them, or a hexagonal coned point like my moonstone. It was some sort of 3D little star with many points in all directions; interlocked pyramids. I picked it up. It moved. Fast. The circle was so wide. "Oh my!" the man at the counter said. "I haven't seen that before. How are you swinging it like that?"

"I'm not. It just moves." I held my wrist with the other hand, trying to prevent any movement of my arm at all. It had been slightly juddering, but my intent had been perfect stillness. The star still swung, right out into a perfect circle. "See? This only just started happening."

He looked at me and picked up a pendulum, and told me it was a red jasper. It moved, forward and back, quite strongly. He looked at me a little surprised. It was a brief bonding moment.

"Ha! That one's for you!" I said, more delighted than I would have expected. I made him try another one, a green one, and then a gold one, and neither moved. We were laughing by now, like two excited children, sharing a moment.

"Well it looks like I need a jasper!" he said. I had found another one, a lapis lazuli, which also started swinging like mad. "That star one you have got is called a merkaba. It's basic quartz."

"What's a merkaba?" It was attractive but it looked to me like something a New Age person would wear around their neck. It looked a like a big star of David.

"We've got books on them. And pendulums probably. And crystals of course. They say the merkaba symbolizes the light body." My face asked for more information. "It is to do with New Age practices of opening the heart, of ascension into higher conscious and of clearing the spirit of old wounds."

"I see." This was the first time in my life anyone had spoken in this way to me, with this sort of information.

"Yes, it's mystics' kind of stuff. I'm not an expert on any of it. I just work here the odd day now I'm retired. Sometimes I dip into the books."

"Well I better have this star. What did you call it again?"

"Merkaba."

"And what is a light body?" I asked.

"It's a tool for travelling into higher planes. Astral travel and distant healings and things. I really don't know too much. But there is so much information out there."

"And here was me, thinking I was far out with starting to become a medium." There. I had told a stranger.

"You are, are you? There are a few good ones around here. They come in and out."

"Really?" I was suddenly thrilled at the prospect of a kindred, especially one with some experience or answers.

"Sure. Look them up."

"They advertise?" I asked.

He laughed at me. "Of course! How do you think they work? It's not the Dark Ages!"

Perhaps it wasn't. Perhaps I was from them and so was almost everyone I knew. I had no idea that good mediums advertised. I thought they were word of mouth, and somehow hard to come across.

"Don't you feel a bit like we are in *Harry Potter,* with the pendulums," I said, "being picked by our wands?" He laughed.

"Yes! I suppose. Look into crystals if you are interested. Are you Hermione?"

"Sadly not! She might have more of a clue!"

"Well I don't know what I am supposed to do with this jasper." His pendulum was swinging. I showed him how mine says *yes* forwards and backwards and then it said *no* left to right. His did it, but in very short little swings.

"Good luck!" I said.

Naturally I was encouraged by my visit to the shop. I gave myself a talking to on the way home about my mind. I thought it was smart. It was clearly smart, and narrow. I was making drama with it about basic communication with the Other Side, when there was clearly much more than I could comprehend being written and discussed in metaphysical circles.

It was time to be confident for as long as confidence could last on this new ground.

I walked into the house and said, "Patrick, if you are here, it is time to learn this. Thank you for your offer to help me. Let's practice and find a way to understand this gift. It needs outlining in some way. I need to understand it or experience it. People keep telling me I'm Hermione and I'm as boring as a common muggle!" I kept my heart high and I genuinely felt lifted. "This is not beyond me. It is all over Barnes & Noble for goodness sake. Now come on."

His voice came from my bedroom.

"I can hear you," he said. "I was reading at your vanity here."

"Reading what?"

"One of your text books. From class. It was on the desk."

"You can read?"

He laughed. It was a pleasure to hear. "I managed to fumble my way through a few scripts, my lady."

"No! I mean you can read my books? How? They aren't, I don't know. They aren't in your dimension!"

"Oh. But they all have a sort of astral version. All objects do. How do you think spirits move things? We can connect to what you think is the physical component of anything. Anything with a basic atom."

"Wow. Seriously?"

"You've heard of cars being moved or turned over in accidents, haven't you? Of random rescues at accident scenes?"

"Yes." As soon as I became self-conscious about being able to hear him, the hearing started to fade. I had to train myself to stop.

"Every time I think I can hear you," I said. "No, that's not right." Communication was key. "Every time I contemplate the strangeness of being able to hear you it starts to fade a bit."

"That's why people aren't mediums. The mind!"

Intellectually the things he was saying made sense. That helped. On top of that, I had to take a leap of faith. It was a mental one. I had to just accept. With acceptance of what I was experiencing, it could become normal, and I would stop this trigger inside me that kept questioning it again.

"So, you are able to read my books when I'm not here?"

"Yes. If I want! I didn't think you would mind." He smiled. He could be sweet as it suited him.

"I don't mind," I said.

"Good. You don't need any more of these books! Class is out for summer!"

"Did you really read academic theory this afternoon?"

"Here's the deal, Jodie. No lies. Ok? Deal."

"Deal. Of course."

"Ok good. I read Lyotard on the postmodern sublime."

I was amused to have him reflect my daily life to me. I turned my accent to a very posh English, way posher than I really sound.

"And how was that, pray tell?"

"You can keep prayin'!"

I was biting my lip not to laugh, holding it in my belly. "For?"

"Freedom!"

"From?"

"This fucking course! What the fuck do people do all day? Sit with the dictionary?"

I only noticed the swearing when I wrote the conversation down.

"Yes," I said. "That, or we get the gist and gloss over it and then talk in equally long words when we discuss it in class to mask the fact we aren't entirely sure what the theory was about."

"Good. I feel less dumb."

"If you worked on that accent you might even sound it," I said.

Secretly I loved the accent from the Southern states. I was not telling him that.

"I'll ignore that comment. I actually understood the word 'postmodern' for the first time when I read this."

Was he teasing me? Pulling my leg? "Do explain it to me," I said.

"You're the one getting a Ph.D."

"Try," I goaded.

"It means something that has been done is being done again. Or written. Written again. Or said. Said again."

And that is when I learned Patrick was more intelligent than he sounded. It was the first or second entry in my journal that I would later circle as a pattern and call the "Tao of Patrick". He could make the complicated simple, and he could do it quickly.

Because of my recent exams, I had read every extensive theory of the postmodern, which was meant to start in literature around the 1960s, by every theorist there was. And none of them had put it as simply.

"Crap," I said. "Do you think I need to ditch this class?"

"You're asking me an opinion? Yep. My opinion is that you are over-developing your mind and under-developing your soul. You have the point of literature. Move on."

"Ok." I felt very guilty about allowing the dutiful daily reading slip. But I had an opportunity here. And it felt exciting.

CHAPTER TWELVE

I told Patrick something clearly. "I need to be able to explain. I need to know how I can talk about this or demonstrate it to people like my family and my husband."

"Okay."

"Do you know how it works? The seeing and hearing?"

"No. I just knew you had the gift."

"Are you ready to tell me what you want?"

"How do you mean?"

"When we first interacted, you told me I wasn't ready to know."

"Oh that. Yes. You are. I want you to prove the afterlife."

"What?" I was a stupid reaction and his sigh was warranted. But the weight of the request was not small. I decided that I had given him enough doubt. "I don't know how to do that," I said. "But here's the deal. I can't keep talking to the people I am close to with nothing of substance to tell them. Proving the afterlife is a lot. More than I feel comfortable to take on. But I am willing to do some research."

"You're sweet."

"Thank you." No-one had said anything of that nature to me for quite a long time. There was simple kindness in the sentence.

"Hey. I want you to know I believe in you. I really do. Otherwise I would not have followed you for two months to get you on your own where you could learn."

"That's what happened?" I asked.

"Yes. Truly. There are few with as bright a light. Mediumship shows to, well, I guess you'd call it people who died."

"Thank you."

"You can do this. You really can."

It occurred to me I hadn't heard consistent encouragement for a while. Everyone around me was stuck in their own rat race, trying to encourage themselves. It was powerful for me to listen to it. I had started to like his kindness and his willingness to speak from it.

"Please, can we see what we can do and try to work out the how? I have been to one or two mediums. I had no idea how they got images and pictures, or how they had become able to see what most people can't. The lack of even a basic attempt at explanation made it hard for me to compute it. I'm that kind of person."

"I understand you. I have been like that at times. How about you go and see a medium. I'll come."

"Really?" A good idea, offered for the second time that day. "That sounds like a plan!"

It turned out that there were indeed several people

in the wider Ithaca area who advertised as psychic mediums, and if you broadened the search to include anyone of the so-called New Age, you'd find at least twenty. I was surprised. I chose one and made an appointment.

As soon as I walked through the door, I was in research mode, an academic again but of a new subject. I wasn't skeptical—that would hardly be helpful—but I was observant. I felt myself instantly shift the pressure of this gift and its mysteries to her. Finally, I had a more experienced person in front of me, who was a proper medium.

Helen was short haired, trendy, not my image of the professional psychic medium at all. I found that I had a stereotype. Not a mean one, but an expectation I no longer needed to hold. I found I had wanted her to look like a hippie, clad in velvet in a room protected by the scent of sage and sheets embossed with moons and suns. I felt a bit let down that she didn't look like that, no unkempt hair or long fingernails or flowing skirts. I genuinely questioned for a fleeting second if the lack of stereotypical garb might make her less likely to be able to confirm or deny Patrick as a real presence around me. In those weeks, I repeatedly had to laugh off some of the old structures of my mind.

Woman to woman, I liked her look. Her eyes were full of sharp intelligence and the blond crop and pink T-shirt told me she was having a happy time in life. It was time to address my thinking on psychics as being people from a vaguely different universe, and I did it there and then.

"Hi!" she said. "Sessions are thirty or sixty minutes. We can go with the flow there. Feel free to take notes." She was businesslike. I liked her brusque confidence. She could have been leading a meeting at Penguin Books. "I'm a psychic medium and clairvoyant. Typically, I let you lead with questions about any area of your life and we will see what comes. I will leave some time at the end to see if there are further messages from the spirit world." This was the patter everyone got, I could tell. "Okay?" She smiled.

I got my notebook out and nodded. My heart was fluttering.

"Great! Good morning, Spirit!" she threw out, almost to the ceiling. It was a friendly, natural call. "Don't worry, Jodie, Spirit is warm around you." There was no performance in her tone, no sense at all she felt she needed to convince me. It was matter of fact. "First question."

What happened next was something I would never have expected. I didn't see anyone. But I heard. No voice, just information. It came then in simple knowing, all sorts of information about her life. It wasn't in sentences. I just looked at her and found I had the same information about her in my mind as though I had been her friend and had followed her life for twenty years. As a result, my own questions went straight out of the window.

"This is not what I was going to ask," I said, "but I am still going to ask if you don't mind."

She nodded.

"Are you in a struggling relationship with a man who was married to a friend of yours, and then they got divorced and they blamed you but it was never your fault at all. You'd barely met him before the divorce, only once in a bar." It did register with me that this might be sensitive information, but I was flooded with it. From nowhere. This was a total stranger and I just had to blurt it out in order to imply the bigger question, which was how did I suddenly know all this?

Helen frowned slightly, somewhat surprised.

"Yes, that's right."

"Sorry," I said. "Your house sale won't go through."

She smiled without teeth.

That message about the house had come out of my mouth before it had gone through my conscious mind at all. I had been a vessel for it. "You don't actually want it to go through do you?" I asked. *Where was this coming from?*

"No," she said. "Not really." Perhaps naturally, she was starting to look a bit frustrated with me. I was on her clock, not the other way around.

"I'm sorry," I said again. "My first question should be an explanation. This is very new to me. I had no idea before I sat down that I would know anything about you at all. It's making me nervous. I genuinely came with questions, not to try to read your private information."

She nodded, thoughtful, and looked over her shoulder as though listening to someone, or perhaps more likely she was silently and calmly calling to someone.

"So, what's your question?" Helen said, not unfriendly, but aware of her time and fee.

I sighed a long exhale of emotion. It was a hundred questions. Why wasn't she throwing her arms round me like an old hippie grandma who would make it all alright? "My question is, what do I do?"

"How long have you been a medium?" she asked, assessing.

"Um . . ."

"I mean actively experiencing and verifying it. Not aware you might be." It was apparent she was connected to the same field of all information that I had just been connected to. I hadn't mentioned anything about it.

"Weeks."

"Damn!"

"What?"

"You're too good for weeks. Someone has blocked you."

My heart started racing. It sounded like more trouble. "What do you mean?"

"Patrick Swayze is standing behind you. My guide

is telling me you know. My guide is never wrong. Not that I have ever experienced, anyway. They'll make you do it on your own before you get your best. That's what he will help you with, getting to that point of best. Or has he already?"

"Patrick? Helped me? You can see him?"

"Of course. We'll get to that. I know why you picked me to visit. The spirit guides who support mediumship, and they are there—trust me, I have done this for twenty years—they will make you do it independently instead of feeding you answers. But they support. They are trying to make living masters of this stuff at this point in time, not just channels. You'll go through your paces."

My heart went through the floor. If this wasn't already paces. . .

"I had no idea I was a medium. I thought I was an academic. I mean, I am. I wasn't seeking this at all."

She chuckled. "Who wants a seeker?" That sentence would stay with me. "A bit like my boyfriend's ex-wife. He was seeking her, he didn't love her. Do you see what I mean?"

I did. Not as a psychic medium who had just been given more information, but as a literary scholar. Whomever does want the seeker?

For years to come, Helen's simple sentence about human nature explained so much about what was to come. And about what had already happened.

"So, you can't be '*why me?*' about him." She flicked

her chin up casually to gesture at Patrick. "You can't."

I was nervous. I needed answers, not more questions. It was a need of my soul. I needed my direction. And I had been trained to think I needed answers to my current situation before I could take that direction. I breathed. Her comment about seeking was both philosophical and realistic to my heart, and it had settled me somewhat. Some of my angst had become acceptance of my situation. I found a new willingness, almost instantly, to just be in this new situation and let what it was all about unfold. That was a small new candle of peace in my heart. But it was not yet also in my spirit.

"My first question before I got that information about you, and I'm sorry, again. . ."

"Why are you apologizing?" she asked.

"It feels like intrusion, just knowing things about you!" Unexpectedly to me, this comment formed a bridge between us. We were starting to regard each other with friendliness. It was on my lips to ask her more about Patrick, even though she had told me not to. But she had other things to say and the conversation moved in her direction.

"You don't know those things about me! Spirit does. You didn't know it before, did you? When you arrived? Did you read my mind? Of course not!"

Helen looked over her shoulder with her ear, craning her neck backwards. Her eyes stayed on me. "You came by taxi then."

Wow. I hadn't said a word.

"See. I didn't know! It's Spirit."

I must have looked uneasy.

"Isn't that what you're here for? Answers? They want me to give you ten more minutes by the way. For your reading for me. Just then, before you came in, I was thinking about the house. They didn't realize I didn't want to sell. To me, even without them," and again she gestured behind her with her ear, "that information coming to you means someone big is guiding you, and it's not just Patrick Swayze. They help with intuition."

"Wow." I was starting to feel a bit overwhelmed. I had just wanted to ask for some clarity about the turmoil in my mind and heart about the right next steps in my everyday life. She was right. I was there for answers. Now she had told me not to ask the question! And we had got on different tracks with our respective trains of thought.

"I'm sorry," she interrupted with. "I just needed to tell someone. How it is. No-one talks about it. The beginning. I know it's the strangest experience you have ever been through. It was for me. They are telling me you're an academic and it's hard. I just don't meet someone young like me very often, or under forty, who can do it too and might be able to talk it through with me. Help me explain to people. Let's forget it. Don't pay for the session."

I had been excited about this hour away from

Cornell, but my heart told me to let her be. I got the impression she didn't bail on sessions very often. Hadn't she readily, and undeniably easily, given me confirmation that Patrick was really there at my shoulder?

"A saint is going to come. I can promise you. You'll meet him." I wrote it down.

Naturally, this decentered me a bit. I wasn't in the practice of saints. Were they a practice? What a stupid thing to say. What I meant was I hadn't much thought about saints during my life. But I hadn't much thought about Patrick either.

My heart was twisting in my chest. I decided to accept Helen's suggestion we let the reading drop.

"Can I pay you anyway?" I asked.

"No," she smiled. "It's bad karma."

I got up to leave. I felt it was a shame I wouldn't know this woman better. But the situation wasn't right to change that.

"Jodie," she said. "It really is Patrick. Spirit says that is on your chest. I don't know why. I know you can see."

"I can't see your guides." I said. I had just realized. I couldn't see anyone behind her that she was talking to.

"Ah. That's because you haven't accepted the gift yet. They see that, and it's not all you that makes it happen. It's two-way."

CHAPTER THIRTEEN

For the next couple of days, I stayed up until two in the morning. I picked the pendulum up again to try to understand how it might work. I practiced seeing and hearing, and the conditions I needed to best see and hear. I wasn't perfect at it, and I was experimenting without a teacher, but I noted emotional and mental changes in myself and whether they had an impact. Class had become a struggle, but I did keep reading as much as I could with a couple of hours over lunch. I had understood Patrick's enthusiasm for the mystical, but I wasn't about to ditch my Ph.D. in the middle. When I was tired, or I was less able with the spiritual things, and when it seemed that I felt bogged down with the intellectual reading, I wasn't in the right frame of mind to make the most of it. It does take two as Helen had said, and mostly Patrick remained either calm or enthusiastic. But he was also determined.

We spent some hours practicing just hearing and sensing words. His ambition was that I would never again need a pendulum. I still liked to pick it up as a safety net because sometimes I could hear him aloud across the room, and sometimes his words echoed somewhere inside me, not always in my mind, but sometimes in my stomach area. I had a hypothesis that

that was when I felt more down or less hopeful. I don't think he had had any idea just how much training would be involved in approaching me. He had thought he was approaching a born medium. Whether I was actually developing the skills of these extra senses or whether we were releasing the old trauma of a natural medium, I wasn't sure. But we practiced a lot.

He willed me words, every day words, for several hours in a row.

"Tell me a colour," I'd ask, and then I'd try hard to listen, and shout out "Green?"

I was watching everything about how I was hearing, trying to mark down every variable. Mostly, I got the answers correct but he would experiment too, sometimes just thinking a colour, sometimes trying to mentally transfer it and sometimes just saying it at different pitches.

Once or twice I lost him, and I'd pick up the pendulum to see a side-to-side swing of no. "Not blue? Damn! Do it again!" I'd shut my eyes, ordering my own mind to shut up. When my own mind was still, I could hear a lot more clearly. "Ok, maroon.'

"You got it!"

"Grey?"

"That's my colour!"

Having clear mental space became the first thing I was sure was making a difference. If my mind was lost in worry on my heart, be it about paying bills at home, or Edward's bemusement with me, or if I was really tired or distracted mentally, I wasn't as good at hearing anything. Patrick felt a little threatened by that.

"You aren't just going to give in and disappear, are you?" he said.

"No."

"You won't go home and forget all about it?"

"No."

Still, I was not looking forward to going home and screeching it from the roof tops either.

I had support from my best friend and from my mum, who was just worried I was doing too much and going in too many directions, as a mum might be. I also finally called her sister Christine in Austria and finally told her all the things on Nonny's list. She had a new apartment and Nonny could describe its closest details. I had never been, but Christine, amazed, confirmed I was right. She asked me if I might be able to talk to the son she'd lost years ago, before I'd been born. He had only been two when he'd died after an accident.

"I have no idea," I said. I hadn't thought about requesting to speak to a specific person who had crossed over, as mediums typically put it, and neither had I thought about being the intermediary for someone else. I didn't feel anywhere near confident enough, especially when I sensed the weight of others' emotions. It would be a lot to try bringing information for someone, not just Christine but anyone, who had a lot of emotional investment that I succeed and get it right.

I kept training. Names, for some reason, were difficult. More so than colours. "Tell me a name, Patrick."

"Lisa?"

"Yep".

"Too obvious, Patrick, I could have made that up. Do it again."

It didn't occur to me how bossy I was being, or how he might have reacted to that. Or even if there might be a better way to do this. I was just driven to get it right and wouldn't give up. I had a nervousness in my gut about being asked to prove or at least demonstrate his presence, and indeed that of Nonny and perhaps others.

"Tom?"

"Yes."

'Peter?"

"No! I never said 'Peter'."

"Ugh! Where did that come from?" I sighed. "Really. No 'Peter'? I thought you said 'Peter'."

"No. Not me."

"Jesus!"

"No."

"I heard 'Jesus'. Did you mean as in a colloquial kind of blaspheming? As in, 'oh, Jesus'?"

"I never said it. I don't think I did."

"Okay, never mind."

I asked him to do so many words in all categories, some of them more creative to get an unexpected answer or association. It got fun the more confident I became, despite the odd curveball. I just stopped trying so hard, which also helped. I realized that in trying so hard I was somehow squeezing my mind to focus as though it were a muscle, and I was restricting myself. Eventually the answers became so frequently right in all sorts of categories that I didn't need to check them with the moonstone, and I stopping having it waiting in my palm all the time.

"Name an actor."

"Tom Cruise" is what I heard. I sensed an image of him in my mind, too. I didn't think I had put it there.

"Do you like him? Tom Cruise."

"Personally?" I was amazed I heard that. I was still amazed by the clear hearing, I really was. I was being methodical, but I truly felt gifted. "Sure!"

"Give me a random name in case I am asked one day to hear one."

"Well, hearing them isn't the same as hearing me, is it? You've tuned into me. My way of meeting you. I don't know if it is everyone's. You don't hear Nonny so much and she visited yesterday. She told me."

"You know her?"

He smiled. "Kinda. She's guiding you as much as

I am. I do cross over to sleep, you know!"

I hadn't got to thinking about his existence when I wasn't practicing. Somehow, I didn't want to ask a lot just then. I was starting to rely on him and I didn't want him slipping away into another world. The less I asked the better. I didn't want to focus on it.

"Good point," I said, feeling beaten by my massive lack of real knowledge. "Just one more name."

"Kathleen."

"Who?"

"Kathleen! From the story."

"What story?"

"About Nonny!" he said. "I liked it. It was well written."

"Thank you."

Practicing until my eyelids scratched on dry eyes, I got to know him a little bit more. I was not sure he was trying to entertain me, but he was. He could be funny, and the things that cracked me up were totally from left field. Some things he said felt considered, others impulsive, all somehow indicative. I wished I had someone to ask about him to tell me if he was being glib or cautious or thoughtful, or simply if this really was him as they knew, no pretense.

"What matters?" is something I remember I asked.

I listened for a while and a few things came. Eventually he settled on "People." One of his options was the single word *Mom*. Another was *politics*. But "people" stayed.

"What's the best thing you did?"

"Live."

"Are you sad?" I asked. "That you're not still alive?"

"Not at this point, no."

"Good. I say happy, you say. . ."

"Love." That was disarming.

"Give me a kind of love."

Instant response. "Real." I could hear all that conversation with crystal clarity. I was mostly sitting over a desk with a pen in my hand as we practiced, but I turned and looked at him. I could see him leaning against the door frame. He leaned a lot.

He spent some time firing back a few questions before I turned in for the night. Occasionally if I asked him something quotidian about himself, he'd ask: "And you?" He seemed interested in my animal stories. I told him I'd been a dolphin trainer for a while in my late teens.

"Horse shit!" That phrase was sticking. The one for feeling pleased was "How do you like them apples?"

"It's true. Just for a little while."

"No way!" he said.

"You don't trust me?"

"Not yet."

The comment about the dolphins was true. But

that wasn't the point. His comment stung, and I was surprised it did.

We were into week three when I felt a hand on my shoulder. I told Patrick that I could feel his touch.

"Go figure," he said, nonplussed. He removed his hand.

"No! I mean I can feel it!" I was stunned, and he was not following me. "As a kid I thought the hands of a ghost would go right through me. I haven't thought about it a lot more."

"I'm not a ghost. I read the book, didn't I? I'm not made of air."

"I thought someone from the Other Side wouldn't be able to touch this side. I thought they'd be cold."

"Do I feel that way?" he asked.

"I don't know. I just registered a touch on my shoulder. I didn't overthink it."

"I haven't thought about it either. I'm no pro. I was an actor not a mystic. I try to get help but it's not always easy. There aren't many mystics just floating about in Ithaca."

I had so many questions. But touch was astounding me. It would mean something solid. A nervous system of sorts. Something solid about the forms for consciousness even after death.

"I want to know how I feel. Do I feel transparent?" He looked perturbed.

"Touch me then."

"Can you see me? Clearly?"

"Yes, clearly enough, most of the time. You look like Patrick Swayze."

"Dumbass." I had noticed that when he smiled or was not tense, he seemed to become more solid before me, and if he was feeling a lot of emotion then his movements would catch my peripheral vision. His visits were not all quite the same. His state of being had an impact on our ability to communicate, just as mine did.

"How many fingers am I holding up?"

"Three?"

"Shit, yes!"

"I can see you," I said.

"Really? Is it consistent?"

"When I look, I think so."

He was totally thrilled by this. I was rewarded with a huge smile.

"Do it again!" he said.

"Ok."

"One finger," I said.

"Yeah! One more."

"Two," I said, smiling.

"You got it! Ok, shut your eyes. Don't look."

I shut my eyes.

"Now how many?"

"Two again," I said.

"Wow!"

"Thanks!"

"You can see me with your eyes closed. Do you know what that means? Sight is beyond the body. I bet if I put my hands over your ears you could still hear me."

"Do it then!" I was intrigued. I had been talking to him about hearing on the inside and hearing on the outside. I had no other way to describe it and it made such little sense to him that we gave up on me trying to explain. I'd said sometimes I seemed to hear his words inside my body, my own shell, rather than from across the room.

He walked across the room and put his hands over my ears. I felt warmth. I shut my eyes.

"You are not for real. You can hear me, can't you?" He was whispering.

"Yep!"

"Do I feel like a ghost?"

He put his hand on my palm.

"No! Oh, my goodness! That felt like skin." The man in front of me was dead. I could see him, hear him and feel him, all with some other set of senses. The senses of the spirit, perhaps. "Patrick. I think you might have made me a medium!"

"Woooow," he said. "Woooow. I'm stunned!" He looked emotional. I was sure in that second that I saw his shirt change, just change in front of me with his emotion to one with short sleeves. It was off white or ivory with a pink stripe, an orange one and a blue one

I think. I was stunned by the change in my vision and didn't know what to do with it. Perhaps I was seeing an associative memory of his. There was so much to learn about the soul. What a world to open to.

"Jodie," he said. "Let's go see another medium. One that you don't scare, hey?"

"Very funny."

"Seriously. Make a booking."

"Alright."

CHAPTER FOURTEEN

I looked through the listings.

"Why do you want to see another medium," I asked.

"To show off!"

That made me laugh. You know when you meet a new person and get to know them and think about their character? You might even look up their astrology sign or their Meyers Briggs profile? Then there's a moment when they are with you and they just put into one expression everything you think you have started to know about them? That was Patrick just then. He seemed happy. The actor, the Leo who wanted the limelight, the showman, the entertainer, the happy go lucky man who had the confidence of having made it behind him. It was an effortless and beautiful confidence that comes only with the recognition of security at a deep level that the world is safe and good. It was a joyful moment for me, his request to show off. It was Patrick fitting his cosmic profile perfectly. It felt true in a deep way. For me, in the readings I have done in the years since the summer in Ithaca, that's what I mean when I say someone is being their cosmic selves. They might not be being their divine selves, but still. The cosmic self-expressed is always a delight to behold.

"Okay!" I found another medium online. He was

a man with a confident advert and good testimonials.

"I'm gonna test him!" Patrick was excited.

"Why?"

"Don't be testy, Jodie. I want to see how good he is! I want to try some of what we have learned."

"Okay, I don't want to break your mood. But can you remember that there's something sacred to me about this gift? I don't know how many bridges there are into the afterlife. Those who can cross them to benefit other people surely need some fondness from you."

"You're a sweet woman! Always caring for everyone else. It's sacred to me too. Doesn't mean I can't goof around! Jeez, I goof around with you!"

"Let's go then," I said, placated. "I wonder if Nonny will come."

"I hope so!"

I had to use my best English accent on the phone and a lot of sweet pleading to get Robert to see me. He was regarded well and he was busy. He asked me what I wanted and I said just to see him. Was I in grief? No. Had someone died? Not recently. Then what? I told him I just needed to see him and that it mattered. He fit me in the day after next.

It turned out that Robert quite liked the testing. It put him in a buoyant mood. He told me he did fifteen readings a week and he called them his "good dead uncle" readings. I was starting to find the lives of these living mediums fascinating. "You know," he said, to explain, "everyone wants to know their good dead Uncle is okay. And that is good. A blessing, Lord, to be of service." Like the first medium, Helen, he looked to the ceiling. I noted this gratitude to the ceiling as a pattern. And why not? These mediums were among the few people I had met who, in front of a complete stranger, practiced open, vocal and happy gratitude for their gifts in life.

Rob was older than Helen, and I guessed between fifty and sixty. He had a real sparkle in his eyes and a seriousness in his posture. He was dressed simply, in a simple room in his home. Like Helen, he had no tarot cards or crystal ball. Just him and the two sides of a naked table. I sat at one of them. There was something enchanting about him.

"Now to yours," he said. "He's a tester! And I like him!"

There was a sort of male bonding courtship between them for a few moments , like two happy cockerels off mating season who had crossed one another in the street. They were assessing one another, sizing each other up. I couldn't actually see Patrick in the room but I could feel him. I just scribed.

"Cowboy boots." Robert said. He looked at me. "Don't say anything. I am talking to him. Don't give me anything! This one is not here because you lost him and you are sad. We are not doing the sad stuff here."

Presumably he was trying to talk to Patrick telepathically. I barely dared to smile. I just noted in small letters to myself: "Testosterone combat: amusing." Patrick was making him work for it, it seemed, just as he tried his best to help me to hear. He was looking for the professional, and likely studying him too. We were interested in how this works.

"Now you're distant. I know," said Robert. "Don't want me to see you. Ok then. I'll find you."

And I swear it was a cat and mouse game. I have learned since how to hunt, for want of a better word, when a spirit is playful like this. But this was the first time I had ever seen it. Patrick was all retreat and provoke like a happy fencer, and with some seemingly magical ability in his own spirit, Rob was able to pursue him.

"Texas! No, no, no. This is not Texas, it's the West Coast!"

I dutifully wrote it down. I admit I was bewitched.

Rob said to me, "Who is this cowboy? He's showing me cowboy gear, the boots and things, and the horse like it's the Wild West. The hat. This hat and another hat. And another hat. And jeans. There are definitely some films but there are all these horses. It's like Clint Eastwood or something if that makes sense."

"Do you want me to tell you?" I asked.

"Do you think I am an amateur?" he chuckled. "Look, Darling, the world of spirit is not a serious and somber place. Some of them are. But sometimes they play and sometimes we do. He's a good person. I can feel the heart."

"Okay," I said, understanding the mood. "In that case I will say that I do not think Clint Eastwood is dead."

"He says he likes them apples. Does that make sense?" He doesn't even look at me for an answer. "Now I have a voice. Definitely American. Some South in it. Can't be a relation to you because you are very British. What are you doing here in America?"

"Studying," I said.

"He says ad infinitum."

"Maybe," I said.

"A ranch. Big. A plane. His, no doubt. Movie star. There's no doubt to me."

This medium seemed to be doing it on his own, without the guides. He was concentrating, reading despite his mirth.

I didn't throw Rob a bone. He didn't seem to need one. "There are a lot of animals with him. Um, Beverley Hills? Not getting this right, am I? 90210?". I knew Patrick was flirting with him and Robert was doing the best he could to interpret from weaker clues. Beverley Hills would give me Hollywood by association, but Rob took it to the old TV series *Beverly Hills, 90210*. "He is saying something now like he has gambled and lost."

That totally threw me, but I wrote it down. If Patrick was a gambler he hasn't mentioned it to me. I shrugged, disappointed at any hint of inaccuracy, but Rob went on: "I'm thinking now *Young Guns*, or something, was that even a movie? I don't know but now it looks like Emilio Estevez and those young guys in the Brat Pack in the '80s; Charlie Sheen and people. You're probably too young to know."

I was too young to know the Brat Pack. But I knew Robert had Patrick under his spell, whether Patrick was willing to reveal himself or not. "Can I ask you a question?" I asked. "Is he stuck?'

"Stuck? No, he's not stuck." He listened then. I saw a cocked ear. "Well to get it dead accurate he is sort of semi-stuck."

"What do you mean semi-stuck?" I thought then of spirits as stuck here on Earth, having missed their chance to go where they could have gone, or should have gone, now tortured and lost and frankly scary. The imagery of stuck-ness isn't good. When I thought of someone being stuck I thought trapped, locked in, trying to flee and not being allowed to. My imagination was awful to me, showing me spirit forms finding it hard to leave bodies, or haunting old places, broken. I could not stand this thought. Semi-stuck was not much better. "How can he be semi-stuck?"

"I'm sorry," Robert cut in. "He just said he sends his love and good night. I hear the Texan now."

"Damn!" I said. Robert shrugged.

"That's Spirit. His prerogative."

"His prerogatives are doing me in."

"Darling, you've scared him. Don't worry, let's sort this out. This man is not stuck. He's either a guide or training to be a guide. That explains why he is not your good dead uncle. He'll be forward and backward. Do. Not. Worry." A pause. "Ah there he is. He says worry is your middle name."

"Okay," I said. My heart was through the roof. "He's like a wild horse sometimes."

"What's Jodie's real middle name?" Robert asked aloud. "Be kind."

"Elizabeth." I heard that in Patrick's voice. He had come a bit closer and then retreated again.

"Yes, that's right," I said.

"He's chuckling.," said Robert. "He cares. Good. He's new to this. Some of them have done this for a long time. This one is strong and young. Young to Spirit."

"True," I said.

"He's happy! He's just, well, you're right. Like an untrained horse. Death is hard on people. Remember that. He's well-adjusted but still feels a mission here."

"Sorry."

"He says if you apologize one more time he is going to put an axe through your head. Does that make sense at least?"

"Yes, that's him," I said.

"Good. You're scared, aren't you?" he said.

"Yes. A bit." I was honest. "This is new and a lot of responsibility that I don't know if I can quite bear."

"He's not stuck in the sense of unable to cross. He's crossed and visits. He's semi-stuck in the sense of not quite knowing where to guide you. It's not a metaphysical issue. It's an issue of him thinking things through."

"Phew," I said. "Thank you. Sorry. I am still not very used to this and all the right language."

"What do you need, Jodie?" Rob said. "Let me help you."

"Do you think you might be able to get his name?"

"Do *you* know it? I've had Presley before. The man had no idea."

"About?" I asked.

"He hadn't practiced his communication. This guy has been doing. He's telling me."

"I know his name," I said. "I'm not testing you. I just. Well, despite everything, I just need someone else who is as good as you to confirm. I still need it."

"Love, you're a cynic. He's here to get that out of you. To eradicate it. Cynicism is not a gift, he says, and to be honest I agree. No, she's not, she's not. Sorry he is saying to me telepathically that you are too rational. I don't agree. You're just not an idealist like him. He had it good. In terms of his consciousness. Until he died. Strong background. Good genes. Good success. Good woman. Not a lot to complain about then bam, cancer, and he was gone."

"How do you . . ."

"Just let me say something. He cares about you. That is obvious. But he is frustrated. By cynicism. My guess is you were hurt as a kid. Is that right?"

I nodded.

"Robert will sort it out," he said of himself. "Now, he doesn't know all that yet. You don't talk enough. He doesn't know what you have been through. You watch. You speak. I think only when you need to. Patrick wasn't like that."

I was startled by this moment to introduce his name.

"Buddy! Sorry, he says his name is Buddy. Let's have a look at you, Buddy."

He closed his eyes. "Come, on, she needs this. Show yourself. Ha." He was silent for a few seconds, rubbing his brow. "Patrick Swayze is your spirit guide. No, he's not. He's your best friend. Let him protect you until you are out of this drama with the academics and things. There's a lot to come. Some doubters, some cynics. A lot of lovers. And by the way, by that, I don't mean boyfriends! Sadly. Sorry, he says you are married. That won't last. I'm sorry for that too. By 'lovers', I mean lovers of what you can do on the Earth and give to others during your precious life. And you must do it. Forget the doubters and tell them that life is the one gift we are given to make the most of God's intent. Then, it's over."

I asked him to repeat that, and wrote it down word for word.

Then I read it back and said, "Hang on, how come? Is it over when we die? You're the medium."

"No, of course not," said Rob. "To be honest, I am not sure what happens. I just know I see and hear them and they verify things all the time."

"Like your shoes! The new ones! From downtown!" I heard Patrick's voice and so did he.

"I got new shoes." I said.

"Do you have a Nonny?" he said.

"Yes!" I was thrilled.

"Well here she is telling me you can do all this so what's the point of you being here asking me!"

Now Nonny had put me in a tight spot. "Verification," I said. "You said you get verification all the time. I need a bit of that. And I am likely decades of ability behind you."

"Fair enough," he said. "This is the good old grandma reading then. Patrick is more interesting but Nonny is sound. I mean in the sense of the purpose in your life. Let's see." His descriptions were clear as day and they were a lesson to me as a medium. The everyday things felt like wonders to my heart. They weren't globally significant, and I already knew the details, but the touch points in the information were almost like I could reach out with my own fingerprint and touch Nonny's over the veil. Rob described Nonny playing cards in a group. She had run a whist drive in her home as an older lady. He talked about her visiting Vienna, where we have family, and even having no tram ticket when the Austrian inspector had come. I had heard that story before. It was amazing to experience the memories she had chosen to bring to him.

"Your Nonny is showing me a necklace, a pendant, and it is gold. It has an angel on it but it embossed or raised on the heart-like shape of it. I can't put it better than that. It either protrudes a bit or goes in but it isn't flat."

"I don't have one." It meant nothing. And it sounded hideous. Not my style at all.

"Well it will mean something. She's a strong lady."

"Thank you." I still felt choked at the mention of Nonny, even though the necklace made no sense. I wrote it off as something a grandma might think was symbolically cute. I think Robert did too.

"Now what on Earth has Patrick Swayze got to do with you?" Robert asked me.

"He's just around." I said. "Has been for some time." That's all I gave him, because that is all I truly knew.

"Yes. And he's happy."

"Good."

I walked out of there buoyed and with a swing in my step. I still had unanswered questions but I was grateful in a true way for what I had been given. Gratitude was with me a lot. I was so relieved Patrick was not stuck. I was so relieved that I was not somehow to blame for anything negative happening to him. I realized that if he wanted to be somewhere else, he would simply get up and walk out of my life.

In downtown Ithaca, I walked around in a happy daze for a couple of hours. There was no way I could sit and read. I window-shopped, bought a coffee, and wandered around the pedestrianized part of the town. In a shop of gifts and jewellery, I stopped and looked in a long glass case, which had many shelves of trinkets and jewels of different kinds. In the middle shelf in front of me was a dark velvet case, standing open. Inside it was a necklace. It had a gold chain and an angel hung from it. Its heart was rounded, breaking the frame of its body with its love.

I didn't buy it. Just looking at it was like a miracle to me. It touched my heart so deeply. How had she known I would randomly walk into this shop and see this necklace? I had made so many choices to get me to that spot in time and space in just that moment. I had not felt guided there. All I knew was that Nonny had made a prophecy and that it had come true. I was overjoyed. I felt a connection of the heart to my grandma that was pure appreciation, wonder, and happiness.

CHAPTER FIFTEEN

Patrick had evidently decided to show up in class. I was sitting, listening, and in the corner of my eye a black T-shirt caught my attention. He stood by the chalk board and used his finger to outline a smiley face. I tried not to react. Then he leaned against the wall and watched for the rest of class.

I was one of the last to leave the classroom. There were about thirty of us, but that day I made a point of being slow to pack up my books. Quietly, I performed excuses to keep me in the room while the other students filed out. I had to tie a shoe lace. I had to hunt for my keys. I had to get my notes in the right order. I offered to be the one to wipe down the tables from a birthday cake we'd had shared as class had begun. We'd had two birthdays in class so far.

Patrick was standing in a bay window of the room, facing in. He was still to the right of the board, leaning against the window frame. He looked inwardly alive. His eyes were sparkling. He had a slight happy smirk on his face. His body was still but his eyes suggested that inwardly, his soul was laughing his head off. For him at least, class had been very fun.

The professor and I were soon the only two other souls in the room. I realized I had done little to impress this particular teacher. I had barely spoken in class since the first and second day. That was fairly easily hidden in a class of thirty for a week or two, but now that we all knew each other it was getting a bit obvious. There were four or five people in the class who tended to hog most of the talking time, and two or three more whose commentary I looked forward to. It was more occasional, but always calmly confident, humble and well considered. The comments suggested the kind of deep reading in the library we were all supposed to be doing and that for the last week I had more or less skipped other than skimmed snippets of the information.

At Stanford, my peers and I could tell if someone had not got through the reading and we tended to cover for each other. This class was different. It was the first exposure I'd had to much bigger classes with high achieving and hard-working students from all over, from the Ivy League to large public American universities to European universities in countries I had never been to. There was constant performance in the class. It never quite felt at peace. I truly believed it didn't occur to this professor that people might skip even a page of reading however intense those pages of high literary theory and philosophy were. She was a gentle and smiling woman and she was not naive. The academic job market was very tough and very competitive. People might work hard for a Ph.D. for ten years in the US and end up working in Walmart with huge student debt and a salesperson's salary. The fear of that was palpable, if fairly well hidden under the training we all went through to deliver presentations with poise. Despite the average IQ in that advanced class at Cornell being over 140, everyone knew that of the thirty of us, maybe two or three would ever get to lecture in the halls of one of America's esteemed universities. Even then, it would be for a wage that might be a third of what someone walking into their first job at Facebook or Google, which were the big companies close by to Stanford. I had known this in an abstract way by reading data on job availability and job applicants each year. But here I saw the desperation playing out in an open field. I had noticed dark circles under eyes in our class, and by now every single person came in with a flask of coffee at ten to nine. I even noticed that a few of us routinely had coffee from the nice coffee shop at the edge of campus that served real coffee to go, whereas some students were becoming pointed about bringing instant in a flask. I knew that was because five coffees per week to go was twenty-five dollars, and the disposable cups versus the metal flasks separated those of us on scholarships from schools with big endowments from those who were doing all this on borrowed help and a loan and a prayer.

I had felt some edge toward me at some of the lunches and afternoon reading groups people had initially set up but that we had mostly then aborted, because reading is best done alone. As though reading my mind, the professor said it how it was. She was about to leave the room, leaving me as the last.

"So, Jodie, we haven't talked much. How are you doing with the class?"

What could I say? The rudest I could be would be to say that I had disrespectfully committed to doing a fraction of the reading because I had become a medium and it was the more interesting to me of the two lines of enquiry. The truest thing I could say emotionally was that I had come to this class to explore a gift and an opportunity and had totally, unexpectedly been presented with another one. And I could add that I was getting a bit overwhelmed by both. She would likely have told me to find extra hours and commit to them both. The pressure in academia is real and the hours are meant to extend indefinitely. Ultimately, I found what I could actually vocalize was something about where I was intellectually on her class. It might be a risk to say it but it was true and I said it anyway.

"I think that it is teaching me that I have to work on something more relevant to living people and more commercial. What I mean is that the more abstract the discussion gets, the less it seems to be able to link back to the world and bring people anything. These discussions about old philosophers are getting particularly abstract and I am not sure how to link them to any object or thing, literary or otherwise."

I had said it respectfully. Patrick burst out laughing in the corner of the room. Of course, the professor did not hear, but she looked at me for a moment or two, thinking.

"You know," she said, "you have a very strong pedigree and all the students in the class are aware of it. You have the privilege of two of the best private universities in the world behind you. Your classmates are expecting great things of you. And in some ways you owe it to them."

I didn't know what to say.

"Be aware of people's attitude. It's not your problem of course. But know your place and what is expected from it. I am looking forward to your presentation next week. As is usual, you'll take three readings and introduce their valances to the rest of the group from the perspective of your academic position."

"Yes, of course," I said.

"I'd love to hear about your time at Cambridge sometime," he said. "I have a professor friend there who I see at conferences."

"Any time. You say when." I was used to a certain informality with professors because I had been educated at places with the privilege of small classes.

She smiled slightly. "I hope you write an excellent Ph.D. thesis, and that our time here helps you." I didn't know if she really meant that or not. I hoped so. But she was calling me scholarship girl, and was also very cleverly masking whether it was brought to my attention an insult, a compliment, or a prod in my backside. "Don't worry about the looks of some of your classmates," she said. I hadn't noticed.

I offered a smile that looked sincere, I think, but that demanded the strongest performance from my heart. She walked out of the door and I sat back down on my chair at the table.

I felt terrible. She had wiped the jubilance out of my heart, and the creeping guilt I was feeling about not performing at the top of my game every day this summer now rolled in on a tidal wave. I felt that perhaps I deserved it. I didn't even want to look at Patrick. I let me forehead thud onto the desk.

"What a load of shit that was to hear!"

"From whom?" I said.

"From her! What a crock of shit!" Patrick still looked so happy. I knew he was learning how to make himself seen to a medium after Helen and Robert, and he was perfectly visible to me. I was feeling crestfallen. "Stop. Feeling. Guilty," he said.

"About what?"

"Do I have to say it?"

I felt like a little girl wanting to reach her hand up to the universal mother. Patrick was unfazed by the professor: "that little repartee", as he later called it, had not affected his heart or mind at all. But it had affected mine. I felt like someone had put me in a snow dome, and had picked it up, shaken it, and put it back down with a thud.

"Yes, you have to say it," I said. I think that was

the first time I spoke in a baby voice in an academic building in front of a dead world-famous movie star. I performed the little girl act with a big, pathetic sigh on the table to indicate we could forget it. But, believe it or not, this guy could see through acting a mile off.

"No! This matters! Stop feeling guilty that you got the scholarship that everyone went for. Stop feeling guilty that this class isn't appealing to you. Or that it was paid for by some endowment from some rich dude like me who just likely wants to let you try this stuff on to see if it fits. These people here are not entitled to make you who they want you to be and put you down for it. It's not okay to let them be entitled to push you around because they think you are privileged and entitled. They don't know you from Adam!"

"I haven't done the work." I could hear him but the guilt snow in that dome I was in was still a storm and not gentle, charming flakes.

"Did you hear what I just said?" Patrick sad. "You get to choose your life. You get to not go to an elective class. This class as I understand is not part of your Ph.D. requirement in California. You get to choose at this stage what you do here. From here on in. Forever. Starting now. Man, this stuff makes me angry! Everyone creeping around pretending to be themselves here! And I'll tell you something else. I want people the world over, not just here, to just stop. To just stop pretending."

There are leagues in the world. People hate to say

it. Perhaps it is true we are all created equal, but it is not true that we all act, think and do equally. Patrick expressed almost everything from a different league than almost everyone I had ever met. A different league of heart and mind. And with the easy confidence of a different league of soul. He had no arrogance with it. I believed that he had taken the proverbial spark of light we are all given and had accepted his, whereas other people are nervous even to pick theirs up and look at it. I wondered if he'd had a life of constantly having to cross a sorry bridge to make connections with average people in average leagues, or if his positivity had protected him and infected others wherever he had been. I felt a real need to pay him a compliment. Perhaps I hadn't done that in all the days he had been around. In fact, I had not.

"You carry a piece of Heaven with you," I said. "You really do."

"Thanks."

He deserved another compliment.

"You're a handsome being in and out." I could see how the in created the out.

"Thanks."

"The things you say and do come from a different place from most people."

"Thank you."

Somehow, his smiles were clearing my mind rapidly. The guilt snow was settling. Melting even. "Of love then, and not of duty," I said. "In terms of making life choices."

He continued to look at me. He looked like he was formed of light. For once I slowed down and really took in the beauty of his face. He had been made in a different place from the average guy on the street, that was apparent.

I said, "Life. Living it. I'm getting your point. I need to be aware each day, of my own heart's choice."

I could have sworn I saw wings on him for a flash of a second. I could swear it. Just a flash.

He was still for at least ten seconds, looking at me. The presence in him almost made me burst into tears. It was otherworldly. It was something inside him that had flashed. Perhaps some spirit inside his spirit.

He smiled and moved, and in the movement he became much more human again. Happy human. It was like light coming into form with action. "Yes. You are starting to get it," he said. "I am doing well!" He walked out of the classroom, right around the group of students congregating to use the room next. "Come on!"

He walked down the stairs, out of the door into the sun over the quad. "Go buy new jeans! Go buy some new black jeans. Or grey instead. Those are nicely faded but they are getting skanky. Off you go! Have an afternoon off."

CHAPTER SIXTEEN

"Come get lunch with us," said Paul. He'd been chatting to a professor and was leaving as I was. "I have to drop this book to someone. Wait here a few minutes? Mike will meet us there."

"Oh, sure." I liked my two new guy pals. We had become friendly. One was tall and athletic, the other was shorter, darker, and more French philosopher in disposition. Both had quick wits and sharp minds. Both had good hearts. We had become a trio outside of class, and walking around Cornell with one on each side of me made me feel protected. Mike, the shorter one, was definitely going to become a professor. He was affable and his readily smiling nature complimented the piercing gaze he gave in class when he was analyzing the soul of an argument. He would do well during interviews to educate the future of America. Paul was likely the sharper of the two, but his brain was so bent towards deep philosophical thought that I didn't think he'd know how to make his ability relevant to the modern "get me an A and a place at law school" classroom. I stood at the classroom building door waiting, watching him move across the quad.

"He wants it so deeply and he's good enough but I don't think he is going to get it." I had felt Patrick next to me before I saw him. It seemed his impressions were the same as mine. He'd been watching Paul in class. I felt much more comfortable talking quietly aloud to Patrick when there was no-one around. To most people I presumed it would look like I was talking to thin air, or at least myself. I did most of my talking to him at the apartment, which is likely why Nonny had waited until I would be alone for several weeks to make her initial approach.

Patrick was watching Paul walk further away from us across the quad. "He'll do ok," I said. "I just hate to see a broken heart. The professors keep knocking his dissertation ideas back, even though he's sharp."

"His heart isn't broken. He's having a great time! He was chatting all class. Unlike someone here! By the way, the professor. You know, I believe you about the abstract shit. You're right, the class is too abstract. People need to say something real to the world."

Paul was returning towards us and I took the opportunity to shift the focus back to him. "His heart is going to be broken. Paul's, I mean."

"He'll do great with the girls!" said Patrick, being light-hearted.

"Yes, he will, but not everyone's first love is in human form. He loves knowledge. He's trying to seduce the university. You saw it. I think that seduction will fail."

Paul was jogging towards us now across the grass, all six foot something of him. "People have to show up and be real. The real them. Then you don't fail." Patrick said. "See you later."

"Ready?" said Paul. "The line will be out the door." Paul worked out a lot and therefore ate a lot. If his mind wasn't deep in the library, it was deep in the menu. Or calling on his signature martini.

"Egg on rye. I'm doing it."

"Jesus, woman! Chicken. Beef. Meat. A girl needs meat. A thinking girl needs meat."

I felt blessed in the presence of men who made me laugh. Paul was one of those men who said funny things in dead sincerity. I enjoyed his company and I trusted him.

We had some easy conversation as we walked over the large quad. It was really more like a small field.

"How's the husband?" he said. "Drawing something?" After his MFA, Edward was almost always with his drawing board while we were at home.

"Likely."

"I still can't believe you're already married! I mean, it's great. But we are still in college."

"We'll be in college until we're thirty-something!"

"Will you have lots of mini yous?" Paul asked.

"He wants children," I said. "But he's not rushing at the moment."

"Don't you?"

"Not sure yet." I said.

"You'll come to the class wine tour and tasting, won't you?" he asked.

"Of course! I wouldn't miss it."

"Come with Mike and me. We'll have a great day.

Wouldn't be the same without you."

"Naturally. Why wouldn't I come? I'm looking forward to it."

"I figured you'd rather go some weekend if the three of us hired a car with Alaina and Jan." Jan was the other woman in class I had spoken the most to. I hadn't got close to many women. Our questions are typically all about the heart as we start to bond, and I wasn't quite ready for that in Ithaca.

"Oh, we could do that too. I'm happy to wine taste any time," I said.

"Ok. You just keep yourself to yourself sometimes. Just checking in on ya!" He threw his arm round my shoulders and pulled me to his side for a friendly squeeze.

The famous old quad of Cornell lead past the university bookstore and then down out through a side entrance towards the most beloved of the sandwich cafes. It was my favourite spot for writing. So far, I had managed two more evenings of writing since I had read from the essay on the nursing home.

People from our course were already filling all the outside tables, waving, joking, looking full of happiness about their new summer friendships. I could see romance forming between some of the people on the course. Crushes were developing. Parties were being planned. Everyone was carrying books, but there was some irreverence in the air. People were getting confident with the subject matter and each other and were dropping their social guards a bit. There was one small round table outside in the corner with a few seats.

"Go grab that," said Paul. "I'll get your egg on rye. Wait for Mike."

I waved at people from our class. The stars of today's three-hour discussion were upbeat and holding court. They deserved it. I found I'd rather observe than join, and from my distance at the small table I could see that some of the women had come alive by force of their intelligence. They had been quiet in many classes, but two in particular were buzzing with a new presence following a good performance in class, and the presence had a sexual energy, a charisma, that was noted by most of the men. It was a happy sight.

Mike arrived, having just met with a professor about his research. He seemed pleased. He came from a film department. His topic was something modern and cool, rooted in academic theory, and because of that he'd get a job. Part of the trick was picking a topic that would appeal at an interview before professors, and yet also to the undergraduate students who we'd be teaching should we ever land a job. Young professors started out by teaching from their dissertation research. Paul's issue was that his ideas would go right over the heads of his undergraduates. He was discussing a philosopher called Heidegger with Mike. On the nature of being. Being versus nothingness. I supposed I had been thinking about just that from a metaphysical rather than philosophical angle.

"You'd have to have read a library to understand you," I said to Paul.

"I hear you. But I don't care. It's this and it works or I'm going to become a cop."

"Either way you'll separate right from wrong, then." I smiled at him. I'd been worried about my new friend, but it was settling to realize that some way or another, whatever the expression, he'd do what he was here to do. I could see the link between the abstract philosophy route on one hand or the downtown cop on the other. They seemed worlds apart, but both pointed to the same kind of comments he made in class. He cared in some deep part of his soul about rightness, and weeding out what was wrong from the perspective of some abstract Truth. It gave me a bit more faith in the universe to think that he'd likely get to his purpose one seemingly random way or another.

"She's right," Mike said. "And it's either this for me or I stay home and watch movies and play video games all day." Either way, Mike wanted to give his focused attention and joy to visual narrative. For him, visual narrative was where meaning was in today's world. In a world we could see as well as read.

It was a knot in my stomach, an instant knot, to reflect silently in front of my two friends about where meaning was currently coming from for me. A world that to most is unseeable and unreadable. To other people's beliefs, it might be nothingness and not beingness. I had no idea what my friends would think of my experiences with Nonny and Patrick if I confided in them. I felt guilty that I daren't broach the subject. Their hearts were good enough to listen and believe me, I thought. But I didn't trust their overtrained minds not to go into fight or flight. I was edging toward seeing the connectedness of things from an intellectual perspective. I just wasn't quite ready to talk.

"Have you seen many of Patrick Swayze's films?" I asked, nonchalantly letting egg mayo drip down my chin.

"Sure, girl!" Mike said. "Who hasn't?" I tried not to smile a smile that would put shame to the sun on a July day.

"Just *Ghost,* and *Point Break* and *Roadhouse*," said Paul, which surprised me. I seriously thought he read hard books and reserved the rest of his time for cute undergraduate girls. "And *Dirty Dancing* of course. About five times."

Mike looked amused. "Five times? *Dirty Dancing*? Dude, do we need to talk?"

"No! Five different women. Five dates. It works a charm. *Patrick Swayze* is my wingman."

"Wait," I said. "Wait. You use that filmic material to get yourself laid?"

"Terrible!" said Mike. "I thought your looks got

you by."

Paul laughed out loud, which was too rare. "I can't dance! You do what you have to, people! I am very good to women."

"You're a scandal!" I joked.

Mike turned to me. "To give credit to the actor if you don't know his work, he's more than a porn star to show your bored date. That's really not the point, despite what this dude here appears to think. I am from a film department."

Paul was still laughing. I had started to laugh too. Mike enjoyed the opportunity to hold court and take the impromptu opportunity to lecture.

"Part of the so-called Brat Pack. Started out there in the '80s. Action. Lots of action. A few philosophical ones. Well known for *Dirty Dancing*, *Point Break* and of course *Ghost* which was a classic with Demi Moore. Almost won awards for playing a drag queen. Even did some Disney I think." He pulled out his phone and started googling. "Mostly a heart throb in the '80s, wait '90s, and also appears to have made a whole load of films I have never seen. And, shit, he's dead! I didn't know that. Did you know he was dead?"

"Yep," said Paul. "Cancer. Last year. I have slowed on the *Dirty Dancing* dates in respect."

Mike looked at him with new interest. "Well. That's kind."

"Let's watch a Patrick Swayze movie, then," I said.

Mike didn't miss even a second. "Well it can't be

Dirty Dancing, obviously, because I don't think Paul is trying to seduce either of us. But I am up for that with a Chinese take-out perhaps. My vote would be *Point Break*."

"Why?" I asked.

"Bigelow. A bit postmodern; a bit of a comment on the 80s Reagan era of capitalism..."

"Oh, shut up!" I said, warmly. "Why else? Not from a text book. From your heart."

Mike looked at me. He smiled like a little boy.

"You're a piece of work," he said.

Paul was chuckling, and calling for a coffee. Mike explained, "Because it is cinema dynamite and it makes me want to eat popcorn. A lot of popcorn!"

"Dude, it's so clear Patrick Swayze never got you laid!" Paul was really laughing, and with glee, at the outright dorky charm of our third friend. Mike the film buff. "Loads of popcorn?" Paul said. "Are you serious? Like a bucket?"

"What does it make you want to do?" I asked.

"Surf!" said Paul. "Take action! Blow up the world! Prevent dark things!"

"I don't like that in a future cop, Paul," I said. "Not the blowing up the world bit. Maybe in a philosopher." But I was intrigued about this film. Other than reading its title amongst tens of others on Patrick's Wikipedia page recently, I had never heard of *Point Break*. "Ok. Someone hire it and I will be at your place at eight." They shared a house for the summer about two blocks from my apartment.

"Yes ma'am," said Mike. "It shall be so!"

"I shall procure one enormous vat of popcorn," I said.

I got up to head to the library, and as I left I heard one whisper to the other, "Where the hell do we get DVDs in Ithaca?"

CHAPTER SEVENTEEN

I left my friends feeling happy. I had a hundred or so pages to read before class the next day and the right thing to do was to go and find a quiet spot in the library. I knew most of the rest of the class would already be there, highlighters akimbo, Post-It notes primed in every colour. I walked into the college store on the way back up the slope, which like Stanford's campus store was a huge space that was officially a book shop but was in fact a retail outlet for everything and anything with the word *Cornell* on it. Sweatpants, T-shirts, pens, bumper stickers, hoodies, baseball hats. At Stanford, we had mock-Tiffany lamps with the Stanford *S*, and dog bowls, and golf caddies, and baby grows. Even little drop earrings. There were several tourists walking around the shop, hunting for gear in their sizes. These shops were not unlike the stores at Disney. Everyone wanted memorabilia to be nostalgic about something they had never been a part of.

I bought a Diet Coke and made myself avoid the rows of new novels on the way out. Of course, the man on the library door caught me with the drink and kicked me back out. No drinks in the library apart from water. Only clear drinks in case they spilled. "Gin?" I asked. He looked at me as though I were a toad.

Fine. I'd walk for half an hour. I would find my

lake at the top of campus. I had jogged it with my iPod two or three times, and I had jogged the first tenth of the route and walked the rest with my favorite songs about five times further than that. It wasn't far from the gym I preferred on campus, which I had chosen because it had classes that kept me going for an hour and because it was different from the gym Paul chose. There was no way I was doing my sit-ups next to him. He'd have laughed at me for the next three days.

I walked up to the edge of the quad, which gives the most spectacular view of Ithaca. At this time of day in the summer, campus was almost empty. To my surprise, I saw Patrick standing, arms crossed, looking out over the view. Ghostlike would never be the right word for the image of him, or for him as I have known him at all. But it's true that the image was somewhat transparent. What was between my eyes and his that was invisible to both of us? Something that mediums called the gateway to the Other Side. I could see no gateway. It wasn't a gate between here and the Other Side. It was more likely some aspect of our greater unused mind.

I kept my distance and observed Patrick Swayze. He looked entirely content, emanating love. He appeared to be gazing happily at a tree. It was a tree in full leaf. He seemed quite delighted by it. As though the tree were enough. In the little time I had spent with him since he had crossed into the afterlife, I had learned that Patrick had a massive character. He had far much more character going on all the time than soul. That wasn't to say he was a man of any little soul as I saw him: quite the opposite. But by contrast to the character, the soul seemed fairly simple. This wasn't the first time I had seen him looking happily and with an easy stillness at a simple thing like a tree. He'd looked the same at the sky, and a cat out of the window of my apartment, at people on my course, and at a pair of women's sneakers on the street. This was just the first time I thought I understood the look. Faced with these simple things, Patrick's soul shone, and his soul was turned toward love. I believed suddenly—or understood rather, because I was certain—that Patrick's soul was always turned toward love. All the time. Watching him watch that tree I felt even from that distance a simple, easy stream of love pouring from his heart. I could tell he wasn't thinking about it; it just flowed spontaneously from him. It had been just the same with the cat. And towards a woman in class after a funny comment. In the sense that a stream does not think about itself, it just flows when it has a path to follow, Patrick's soul just naturally flowed love in all directions. I imagined that those who had known him for a long time had been in the presence of this loving warmth a lot, especially when he was at peace. The character by contrast, was another story. I see character as a series of habits, signals and learned ways of being that mask the soul. There might be whole books on Patrick's character.

Where his soul to me had just that minute become easy to render, the character was, well, keeping me more on my toes.

It might go like this, and indeed it had some evenings of snatched conversation when I had my journal open.

Attempt 1.

Me: "Patrick, what's it like to die?"

Patrick: "I'm not answering that. Lisa would be sad."

Attempt 2.

Me: "Patrick, what's it like to die?"

Patrick: "Who cares?"

Attempt 3.

Me: "Patrick, what's it like to die?"

Patrick: "Boring."

Attempt 4.

Me. "Patrick, what's it like to die?"

Patrick. "Are you suggesting I died?"

With that latter attempt, number four, he had he nicely performed a certain suspicion of me, as though perhaps I was quite stupid. He had been standing there, talking to me, hadn't he? He therefore still had some beingness. Beingness enough at least to be a big pain in my backside that day.

Of course, his character had worked out my plan that evening. I am a researcher, a scholar. Naturally, a visiting vocal and sometimes eloquent dead person had piqued my interest. I wanted to know what it was like to die. He had told me, after all, to buy more journals. That character of his had sensed I was seeking official comment when I had sat at the apartment with a pen in my hand. It seemed to fear an official response on the experience of dying and death. He was self-aware when I had a pen in my hand, quite different from how he looked just watching that tree on Cornell's quad.

"No comment," he had said.
"Ugh, Patrick!"
"I don't wanna be the spokesperson."
"Patrick. I am not the *National Enquirer*!"
"No shit. I like them apples."

There had been lots of frustrating cloak and daggers on this topic of death. His character had edges, as all characters do. I thought there might be an emotional need in him not to talk about suffering to me or to anyone else while he was desperately trying to link me to mediumship and research.

Watching him look over the vista from Cornell that day was different. All I could perceive was the soul. I realized that love poured from him every time he encountered anything that appeared to be in its natural form. And I mean natural as it gestures toward Natural with a capital N. He flowed with love whenever he was faced with anything that appeared to him to be in a state that was meant, or aligned to some higher intelligence on whatever that thing was. In that moment, that thing was the tree. The bridge from his character to his soul was that divine or natural presence that got something closer toward where and how it was meant to be. The tree was clearly doing something very right to his perceptions and I was grateful to it. Indirectly, it had taught me what I had suspected but could in no way give word or concept to. That Patrick's soul was pure love. Perhaps the true soul of everyone is.

This was the first time in over three weeks that I approached him unawares. Up to now, it had always been the other way around.

About eight feet from him, still unseen, I said, "Hi."

The spirit turned. The face smiled. "Hi."

"Nice view," I said.

"I don't like Cornell," he said. "It is full of dead people."

I looked around. I couldn't see any.

"People don't live here. They are asleep awake. I watch 'em." He was full of stillness this afternoon.

"Do you think that about Stanford?"

"Less so."

"Hollywood?"

"No."

"Well you would say that. Perhaps you are career-biased."

"Maybe." There was the slightest touch of

antagonism in his tone. There was invitation in it too. For sparring.

"It's the summer sessions right now. I am guessing the atmosphere would be entirely different if the normal Cornell students were here. Same buzz and brilliance as Stanford. No-one here right now is on home ground."

"Shit, and I thought I was thinking deep. Yes, the view is good. Lisa would love it. It's romantic and she likes romantic."

"What did you mean, 'asleep awake'?" I asked.

"I mean they aren't pursuing their cause. Their mission. Their *je ne sais quoi*. Except you. You are starting to try to at least. You have egg on your face, by the way."

Well that wasn't embarrassing. Much. "Literally Patrick, or metaphorically? The egg, I mean."

"Both, idiot! You're funny, you know. You could go far."

"You think my cause is being here at Cornell?" I felt a shot of fear go through me. Was my cause really that library, which wanted to keep me and my Diet Coke out?

"Hell no. Your cause is gonna reveal here. I was always intuitive like that."

My core was telling me that was true. He struck a chord with me when he said that, but I could not see how it was going to happen in the next two weeks. That made me nervous. I didn't want to talk about it. I was in a good mood after my lunch and I wanted to stay out of confusion for the afternoon so that I could read clearly and make a contribution to class tomorrow.

"I think this view would be better at night," I said. "With all the lights over the town and the moon."

"True."

"Maybe you should bring Lisa to see it."

"And how do you expect me to do that?" he said. "She can't see me, you know. Lord knows, I tried."

"In her sleep," I said.

"Huh?"

"Why don't you do it when she's asleep?"

"You think that's possible?" he asked.

"I don't think it is impossible. Who knows what happen when we sleep. Don't people believe in astral travel and things like that?"

"I need to go!" He said it with urgency, as if to make me go away, but he didn't move. He just turned and looked back over the view.

"Go where? You haven't moved."

He chuckled. "Sorry. That was rude. I mean I need to be with my thoughts. Based on what you said. What if it's possible?"

"Oh. Course it is. Everything is. Welcome to university land. I know you aren't big on this university thing. But for me universities are where everything becomes possible. For you, Hollywood is where that happens."

He looked at me with hope in his eyes and, I thought, nerves on his heart. "Thank you."

"I'll leave you in peace. I'm going to walk the lake, then go read all afternoon."

"Ok. Be careful. Jodie, I probably won't be there tonight. When you come home. To talk."

"Oh, that's quite alright," I smiled. When he was vulnerable and positive at the same time he was very likable. I decided to tease him. "I have a date tonight anyway."

"Huh? What about Edward?"

"No, you idiot! With you!"

He looked as confused and forlorn as a little boy who had lost his fire truck. "I'm going to see if I can find out more about dreams."

It hurt my heart to see his bafflement. I had been warned before about the English deadpan tone with Americans. It was one of the things that sometimes got lost in translation. "Okay, okay. I'll explain. I am going to see my friends Mike and Paul, and I am taking popcorn and we are watching *Point Break*."

If only I could have recorded the face I got in return. It looked like *Point Break* was a ghost and not him. Like I had said something from so long ago in his recall that it took him several seconds to get there. I had seen the same look on my paternal grandmother's face in her nursing home when she had tried to place my face after months away.

"Why?" he said.

"I meant a date with you on the screen! As in we are going to watch one of your movies together. The three of us. Patrick, are you ok?"

"No."

"Why?" I was worried about him suddenly. "Come back!"

"Sorry," he smiled, more present. "For a second there I had completely forgotten making that movie. It took me way back. Wow, time passes. Bodhi. I liked him. He was fun to play. Tough on the knees. Donny will like it that you've seen it. He helped."

"Donny? Oh, your brother!"

"Yeah. Go have fun!"

I turned to leave him to his thoughts and his view. I didn't know when I'd see him again. Or if. I didn't let myself have that certainty, that he would keep coming back.

"Oh, Jodie? Did you tell your friends about me? Me coming to you as a medium? Do they know?"

"No."

"Okay." He turned from me to the view.

CHAPTER EIGHTEEN

We watched *Point Break* with a bucket of popcorn. I don't need to write about how strong an actor Patrick was. His gift would be readily apparent to anyone who watched a few of his films. This one was another contrast to all the ones before, and showed his range. He seemed to like playing strong outsiders who had perspective and leadership to bring. I ran this by Mike and Paul, who had seen more of the movies, and I got some traction on my hypothesis. Johnny Castle in *Dirty Dancing*, Sam Wheat in *Ghost*, Bodhi in *Point Break*. Likely Vida Boheme in *Too Wong Foo, Thanks for Everything! Julie Newmar*. James Dalton in *Road House*. Max Lowe in *City of Joy*, which Paul remembered he had seen. I enjoyed reflecting on Patrick's work with my friends. I had enjoyed watching *Point Break*.

As Patrick had stated, I didn't see him that evening when I came in, and it was quiet the next afternoon too. I had been left to do some reading and prepare for my class presentation.

On a whim, I decided to try to respond to Christine's idea about her son. I didn't have Patrick there, I could feel and see that. But it might be good to try without him around. It was family after all. I would go back to basics with Nonny and try to show my mum and Christine over Skype how the pendulum moved and how it had all started.

I didn't think Nonny was around, but I lit the white candle on the kitchen table, I put the pendulum and my wheel of letters on the table too, and then I went back to sit at the desk in the hall. I called my mum and asked her to come online and to get Christine online too. I asked them to give me ninety minutes.

After forty minutes, I felt Nonny's presence in the living room. I practiced sensing again. I was behind the door in the hall. I could feel a presence arrive, and as I sat still and felt into it, I could feel it was feminine and that it was her. My heart started beating rapidly. How strange when I had had my grandma in the next room so many times before she died, and now her presence brought my adrenaline. I thought of the poem I had read at a couple of funerals that begins, "Death is nothing at all/I have only slipped away into the next room."

"Nonny?" I called. We would see if she could hear me talk loudly from the next room without a pendulum and without another medium present. "Nonny, if you can hear me can you come back in fifty minutes to talk to Christine and Mum please? I want to show them the pendulum. And also, maybe Christine might be able to talk to Michael. I don't know if you see him at all now." He had died so many years before her in Austria, her grandson, aged two. "I'm going to just finish this reading now and I'll be there in fifty minutes at the table. I'm not coming out just yet."

I let my eyes travel to the door between us. There was no movement towards it. Within a minute, I felt that her presence had gone.

An hour later, after technical issues, I was sitting at the small kitchen table with a video Skype link connected to both Vienna and Yorkshire. I had shown the sisters both the letters I'd drawn and the moonstone. Nonny had been present again five minutes before her allotted fifty.

On Skype my mother surprises me. She was instantly accepting, talking over the Skype to the presence of Nonny, who she could not see or hear, with just as much comfort as if she were still alive. She was upbeat and jokey, just like she would have been to Nonny's face. There were no tears, and there was no questioning of me as the link, Christine was more contemplative, serious about it. She pushed on the answers I got from Nonny, very clearly processing the implications of Nonny's swift answers. It was more her nature to question, but she did it kindly. I knew what she was going through. Facing a spirit visitor is a big mental and emotional hurdle.

After a while, when they were both comfortable and both satisfied in their own ways that Nonny was really present, my pendulum spelled out M-I-C-H-A-E-L-I-S-R-E-A-D-Y. I wasn't practicing "tuning in" to see or hear them. I wanted the sisters to see the pendulum move so they could be a part of it. I had the camera on the pendulum and my focus was on it and them.

"Christine." I look at the screen. "She says Michael is here."

"Ok," she says, barely audible over the "You're joking!" from my mother in Yorkshire. I could see there was suddenly a haze of fear between us. Hope and fear.

The presence around me shifted. It was such a subtle feeling but it was definite and hard to pinpoint. It was a bit like seeing someone who has had a mustache for ten years and has just shaved it off. You know something is different. Your senses are firing to your brain that something has shifted. But even though it's staring you in the face you just can't make yourself see it. The atmosphere had just changed in the Ithaca dining area.

The pendulum wobbled. Then moved gently. The word was H-A-L-L-O. With an A. German. I told Christine but she could see. Mum and I were silent. Christine's voice changed and she said, with an Austrian accent somewhere between a word and a whisper: "Hallo." I didn't know what was going to happen. I didn't know what to ask. I just held the pendulum steady and looked down.

And he spelled, letter for letter: "Meine Mama hat Bauchschmerzen."

This is about the last thing I could have imagined

he would say. This much German I knew. *My mummy has stomach ache.* I was startled.

"Christine. Have you got tummy ache?" I saw her look down as though her stomach was some alien thing she needed to reconnect to. "Yes I do, actually." She looked so confused. My mum had said nothing.

The pendulum was moving. A-R-Z-T. *Doctor.* I said it aloud, translating for my Mum. And then the moonstone gave me letters that brought me a chill. S-I-E-K-O-N-N-T-E-K-R-E-B-S-H-A-B-T.

"His grammar is wrong." It just came out of my mouth, and it was a blessing since it was a shock absorber. We say odd things in moments of shock.

"Well he was two and half!" Christine said. She must have understood the message. *She could have cancer.*

"You didn't mention you are ill!" Mum said.

"It's no big deal," Christine answers, pushing her off verbally. I was staring at the page. I had really not expected this.

Christine said out loud: "Wie gehts? Bist du okay?" My mum was silent. I stayed silent too.

G-U-T. J-A. *I'm fine. I'm okay.* Mum sighed an emotional sigh. I guessed that in her mind she has just revisited the news from thirty years ago that her little nephew had died. I couldn't read Christine's face.

M-A-M-A-W-E-I-N-E-N-N-I-C-H-T. *Mummy don't cry.* D-U-B-I-S-T-H-U-B-S-C-H. *You're pretty.* I told her and she screwed her face up.

"Hardly, I'm past sixty!" But she is actually. She's

a good-looking woman, whether she thinks so or not. And she was teary.

"Can he remember anything from when he was alive, Jodie?" My aunt looks at the screen and it seems to me this was her last defense, the reserve on accepting this.

"I don't know. Ask him in German." She does.

"Michael kannst du etwas erinnern . . ." I put my hand up to stop her. The moonstone was already flying in my hand. I was writing down the letters.

S-A-G. . . "Say," we all said. I was praying. I don't even pray, or rarely did then. I watched and read her the sentence after the pendulum was still.

"Ich liebe mein blauen Teddybar." I looked at her. My mum shut her eyes. *I love my blue teddy bear.* Blue?

Tears. The tears just fell. From all our hearts. Just seeing them both, I knew this bear was real. The pendulum was still. My aunt was wiping her face on the back of her sleeve. I so dearly wanted her not to be alone. "I can't remember now if it was actually a teddy shape or a stuffed animal kind of teddy. But he took it everywhere, every single place we went he walked about with it dangling down from his hand. Wouldn't put it down. And yes, it was blue."

I was biting my lip. Hard. I didn't want to cry in front of him and upset or confuse a little boy.

"Nonny, give him a hug," I said aloud. She likely already was.

Not long after, Nonny said they were going now. I was left with an image of grandson and grandmother walking off together hand in hand. Where were they going? To Heaven?

Forty-eight hours later Christine emails me. She had been to the doctor. She had to have her kidney removed.

Thank Heaven, she is now alright.

CHAPTER NINETEEN

I called Edward in tears. I had been so moved. I told him what had happened and he told me he wished he could give me a hug. I explained emotionally that not only was this research fascinating and, I thought, really important, but it might change lives. Emotionally and psychologically, definitely. But what if the message about Christine might help her avoid serious illness?

Edward could hear that I was in the process of deciding I had to pursue this ability, despite my fears. Yes, I feared all the rejection that Patrick had tried hard to heal from me with his counsel. I told Edward that and perhaps he bristled. He chose to read it as another man in the role of healing his wife. I had chosen to see it as what it was to be: a man bringing goodness from his perspective to someone who was willing to grow in return.

My point was this. Maybe I had a moral responsibility to help people with this gift. He didn't baulk at that. He was a big believer in moral responsibility. But if I made the decision to pursue mediumship further, he didn't have a lot of choice in the likely change of my focus in my life, or in the kinds of topics we'd discuss. He knew I'd likely get a hard time from some people we were close to. In that, he already felt emotionally thrust into the world of mediumship and all the cynicism that surrounds it in some circles. That had not been his choice and would not have been his choice. It was hard. It truly was. The conversation we had was softly spoken, and yet distance was growing between us. The change in me would bring change to his life, whether he liked it or not. I was not sure on my side how he was going to respond to that, but he was at choice at least in that. So far, it was not clear. There was nothing mean about him. Nothing at all. He was a lovely human being, and still is. But I didn't know if he was ready to be as flexible as I needed him to be so that I could still feel supported by my husband during this massive personal change.

"How does it work?" he asked.

"I don't know."

"You don't know?"

"Obviously!" Putting an academic in a position where they know you know they don't know the how, is about the most uncomfortable thing you can do to them. It's like being caught naked. I had found this constant intellectual challenge attractive in Edward, but just then it was annoying.

"So Nonny talked to Christine and Linda through you and the pendulum?"

"Yes."

"And she brought Michael to talk to Christine from. . . ?"

"Well I don't know. Heaven?" He was making me sound ridiculous. "I don't know it all, Darling. But thank you for your support," I said. "You know, I am playing emotional and intellectual catch up too."

"I am supportive!"

"Really?"

"Yes. Really," he said. "I am supportive. Nonny won't let you down."

"You're right," I told him. "She's stubborn like you."

Patrick returned the next day. I had just over a week before I was due to fly back to San Francisco. He didn't offer an introduction. He found me in the kitchen and just started talking his purpose.

"I want to try something." he said. The shirt was the same. The hair was longish at the back, more *Dirty Dancing* than *Ghost*.

"What is it?" I asked.

"Sit on that wooden chair and keep still." I had no idea what was coming but I did it. I had only been tidying the kitchen. I just sat there. Instinctively, I closed my eyes. The chair had a lot of space around it. I was facing the open door to the small hallway and my arms are limp at my side, my head hanging slightly. I was relaxed, I noticed. I trusted him.

There was pressure on the outside of my right hand. It was stronger than before, and maybe slightly warm. It felt directed, focused. It was a strange sensation and I just let it be and felt it. Then the same came to my palm, pressure with a push to it that made my hand almost uncomfortable in its place. I had learned by now that over-focusing on a whisper or image made it harder to grasp it, so with intent I tried to absent myself, and focused lightly if anywhere on my other hand. The pressure on my right hand increased, not quite a squeeze but a pressure with weight to it and some strength. A month ago, it would have been from thin air. Now all I could think was that it was from Heaven. I willed myself not to speak, not to move, and to make my body limp. To remain passive. I had not yet learned just how much that helps with mediumship for beginners, but it felt natural to me and so I did it. The passive state makes us receptive.

Slowly, how I have no idea, my right arm began to move. It was lifted silently and smoothly upwards. It was such a shocking and unexpected sensation, both a dragging upwards and a push. I was one hundred percent positive I was not moving it myself. It felt moved from without not within. I knew it. The arm came up and stopped so it was held perfectly straight out next to me. I could feel it being held. Literally. My heart raced and my eyes shot open. I looked, having to confirm what I had just felt. I stared at it, incredulous and it just dropped lifelessly to my side. My mouth opened and as I was forming a *woah* in response, I saw him standing off to my right. Patrick Swayze. There was no question. His expression was one of utter shock, and he was looking at my hand while he leapt away from me. I had moved. I had been moved, literally moved.

He said, so clearly, "Holy fuck!"
He did it again. It was amazing. I was captivated by the possibility it, and truly felt safe.

"Why are you doing all this?" I asked him.
"Because I want to."
"But why?"
"Because I am."

CHAPTER TWENTY

June was looking at me hard. I wondered what she was seeing. It's natural to wonder this with mediums and anyone who professes to have a connection. Was she just seeing blond hair and a black T-shirt, eyes with too little make up today after no sleep, and my pendant on a silver chain? I wondered if she noticed the angel wing round my neck. Perhaps it would signal something inaccurately. I didn't want her to think I was a long time Christian and churchgoer who was into angels and spiritualism and would therefore find being in this class a walkover. I wanted her to think that I was new to this whole spiritual thing and therefore I might be worth some encouragement and praise. Actually, I'll be really, really truthful. I wanted June to think I was new and brilliant. I needed support. My heart was hoping she'd say one thing, any small thing, which would honor what had happened to me so far in Ithaca. June was a medium, teaching a class of new mediums. This was a chance to reveal my secret, a secret that was starting to weigh on me. I could reveal it in a space of non-judgment and validate it. I was practically twitching with excitement just as much as I was dreading failure.

People had arrived, mingled for a few minutes, poured water and shared their snack offerings. I had a handful of nuts and was perched on the end of one long sofa. We were in a private home, twelve students and the teacher all stuffed into a living room full of windows that was as hot as a greenhouse. There were four men, and the rest were women. This class had been Patrick's idea. He had seen the flyer in the store that sold pendulums and crystals and had told me to go. The medium, June, had flown in from California. She appeared to be touring and teaching to promote her book. After her introduction about working with Spirit, which was forty minutes of personal story, all of it riveting to me, June explained she would read for everyone in the room if it felt right to us all, and that some of us would also be invited, or rather called upon, to try to read. There were shy gasps in the room when she said that. June was held in great reverence by her students. They made quiet comments that they would never be able to do it. While they had been in training classes with her before, and deeply hoped for contact, there was still a lot of doubt as to whether the gift of mediumship could really be taught. I was wondering about that when June singled me out with her gaze. She stood at the front of the living room, surrounded by her books and her guitar. She cocked her head as she looked at me, ever so slightly. "You should have a go."

Her eyes travelled down to my stuck-on name badge, covered partially by hair. I moved my hair so she could read the name. "Jodie, that's your name. Jodie with an E." She regarded me as mystics do, seeing more than others see. June was likely seventy-five and she had been a working psychic since she was a child. She had bobbed black hair and was wearing bright turquoise and a big brooch of a parrot. Her reading glasses were hanging on a bright blue cord around her neck.

I wanted her to see my new spirit friend, Patrick. I mean, come on. I had been to a medium to check he wasn't stuck or anything. I had gone to painstaking lengths to prove to myself it was really him. Now, I had accepted it and we were friendly, finally starting to understand each other. Wasn't it fair that I wanted everyone to see him and think I was perhaps the coolest person they'd ever had in class? Some Show and Tell class! *Here ya go everyone, you brought a cheese dip and I brought Patrick Swayze!*

"Have you ever read before?" she asked. That comment was also typical mystic, as I have come to know them. See all, say what is necessary.

"No, I haven't read. I mean, not really." And the blood was rushing around my head. It was strange because there were under fifteen people in this room, and from quiet introductions all seemed friendly. There was no stage and I had spoken in public quite a few times. I didn't mind it. But suddenly I experienced an odd feeling, a bit like the sensation of butterflies in the gut or the heart beating faster and faster. Except neither of these was actually happening. It was the same sensation as that if you can imagine it, but it was in my head, slightly back from the top of my head and round my ears.

June beckoned, looking at me. "Come up here next to me and have a go with someone."

Suddenly, my gung-ho spirit was swallowed by my soul. Pragmatic, ready to give a lecture at Stanford or something. Patrick was often at my shoulder in public and my body turned to look over my shoulder, trying to help my soul out. It was ready to ask Patrick as though he were my trusty assistant, clipboard propped and handy tools ready, "How do I do this again?" I had come to expect him to help me out in this situations with Spirit as though he had been a medium himself and not an actor.

He was having none of it. Zero. He walked into the back of the room through a sliding door, and stood against the glass, leaning with crossed arms. His shirt sleeves were rolled up once or twice. The shirt was pale gray. The jeans were pale blue. Satisfied with himself, he gestured me to my place at the front of the room with a happy little flick of the hand. *Off ya go, Kid.*

I did stand and move to the front, but what I had just seen was totally amazing. Patrick had not walked *through* the door. He had walked through the door. I couldn't remember having seen him enter or leave a room before. How did spirits enter rooms? I had the idea somewhere in my soul that maybe they walked through walls and solid objects. Maybe they sometimes did. But Patrick, I can vouch to you and other mediums, had opened the glass sliding door, had walked in, closed it, and leaned against the glass. A perfectly normal action for anyone alive. But Patrick had died and he had just done the same thing. I was astonished. I felt I was witnessing miracles. I didn't have a context. I didn't know mediums who taught and could tell me what was normal or was not. I was getting to the point that I needed, *needed*, body, heart and soul, to share the information of what I had been seeing, hearing and doing in Ithaca. It was getting too much for me to contain. I felt I wouldn't survive with keeping it all in. My mind was starting to complain. Finally, I felt it surrender. We would share the story. I had to, for my own health. I'd burst.

I stood next to June, obviously unable to tell Patrick aloud what was happening to me. That strange feeling was getting stronger. I couldn't call it nervousness since I knew that sensation. In fact, when I got up and turned to look at the middle-aged women looking right back at me I did get a strong shove of *their* nervousness. They didn't know what would happen. I was a novice. What if I messed up or failed? I could feel these total strangers worrying that something awkward would happen. I had thought it would be easy now I had my easy sight and hearing of Patrick, but no. There was this strange and new tickling at my head and all I could think was that I was going to screw it up.

"Good girl," said June. "Now sit."

"No." It was Patrick. He startled me.

I looked at him. He was behind everyone, and behind the furniture. I didn't know if June had noticed him or what she saw compared to me. I have since learned that different mediums have different skills that go with the gift. Some only hear the Other Side. Some see images in their mind. Some see and hear someone across a room. Some only seem to see if they set a special intention, or a sacred space with a candle. Some have guides to help them when they are paid to read, and I understand that is most common. I didn't know if June could see Patrick or if she had heard him say "no".

She had.

"What did you say?" she looked up and then around. She had heard him. She looked around the room rapidly and finally her eyes stopped at the place he was standing, but she squinted at him, peering, as though he might be hazy to her vision.

"You can't have her do it yet." His voice was very clear to me.

"And why not?" June asked. The class looked around them. Only one woman, one of June's students, kept her own stare at the French doors.

"Patrick Swayze," she said, in surprised recognition.

"Oh shucks!" he said. "This was meant to be fun! You don't do it that way. Just speak!"

"Which way?" I said, as calmly as I could.

"They are trying to be channeled. I don't dig it. June, you need to tell them, the spirits I mean, no channeling. It's tough on the spirit of the living. They basically kick them out of their body."

Suddenly I knew what I was experiencing. I was experiencing someone's death in my own body. Their cause of death. Patrick could see something was going to go wrong.

"June!' he insisted.

"Enough," she said quietly, ready to move back to her class. I believed in June and her story, I really did, but Patrick was very annoyed. Evidently, they could at least hear each other.

"No! Not enough!"

I was listening but I was quiet because I was having a very, very odd experience. I could see green eyes just in front of my own eyes, looking outward. Then I could not hear Patrick at all, or see him. He just disappeared from the room as though vanished into thin air. Then I felt a pain in my chest that somehow didn't feel like mine. But the pain was real. And my ears were still ringing.

I found I could barely hear June. I looked at her and she was speaking quite calmly, but I could barely hear her.

"Deaf! Jodie, deaf!" I heard Patrick's voice before I saw him swimming back into my vision. "He was deaf" I didn't see but could feel Patrick willing me to say it. I could feel the force of him across the room.

"He was deaf," I said. "And African American. And he prefers to be called black than African American. And his mum had green eyes." I could not breathe. I felt like I was going to die, like the air was being sucked from my chest.

"Yes, and he died of a heart attack, June, didn't he?" said Patrick. "He told me outside."

"Yes, that's right," said June. "Spirit said he did."

Who was Spirit to June, if not this man Patrick was talking about and, I was gathering quickly, I was feeling? I couldn't get away from the feeling of his death, and the smell of smoke. I knew he smoked and uttered it, and I knew his death. I could feel he had had a kidney infection too. I shared all this as loudly as I could without keeling over.

The class was amazed. June was standing there confirming. But no-one noticed that I was about to keel over. I could feel myself going down, about to fall. They were just impressed by the correctness of what I was saying according to June. I couldn't express that I could no longer breathe. This man's sensations were all around me and I could barely speak through him.

Thank God. Patrick noticed. I couldn't see him. But while my body was standing, my mind was keeling and my heart was failing.

Suddenly I saw him approach from my left. Patrick came into my peripheral vision from the left. He reached just inside of my left hand and yanked hard. I saw a man move away from me, an overweight man with dark skin and glasses, and a hearing aid battery behind his right ear.

"Oh, my goodness!" said June.

Patrick ignored her. "Did you die of a heart attack?" he asked the man loudly.

"No, I was shot."

"In the chest?" he asked.

"Yes."

I was reeling. I moved towards my seat and went to drink water. Suddenly, the sensations totally shifted. As I drank some water, I regained power over my own sensations.

I did not want to explain what had just happened to the class. I was shocked and embarrassed. They were looking at me like I was a heroine. But Patrick had never put me through anything negative at all. Neither had Nonny. I was stunned this could happen, and that I hadn't seen it coming. And I never wanted to happen to any medium, ever. I had just felt what it feels like to be shot in the chest. What if being a medium for people would be like experiencing ten deaths a day? I wanted to protect them all.

"There are some," June said, "who experience what Jodie just did. They physically feel what Spirit is saying. They have off sensations and must realize it's part of the reading. The spirits will move if you tell them to."

"No," I said. "I don't think they would." I didn't

like to talk back but I was fierce about what I had just experienced. "I know two things from that. . ."

"You're a medium!" quipped a guy at the back. He almost looked envious of what had just happened to me.

I ignored him. "Firstly, I know that I was not able to speak out loud much. I had to fight for my voice. I felt like I was going to pass out. Secondly, that gentleman wanted to be here to have his chance to speak. He wasn't going to just move. I could feel his emotions too. And taste the smoke."

June came and stood behind me told me it was okay. She put her hand on my shoulder and told the whole class about sacred space. She shared that before a class she would bless the room, place roses, call angels, pray for good. She added that she had done this but that she didn't have many "physical mediums" in her class. I felt calm again. Patrick had returned to the back of the room to the door but he didn't look comfortable. June explained to her students what had just happened. She referred to Patrick as my spirit guide and did not use his name. She said he was protecting me from his own position on Spirit and mediumship and likely always would because he was strong. She was very calm and collected. She had been dealing with the Other Side for years.

"June," he said. "Bless you. Thank you. I just think if you could encourage people here who have passed not to come in proving themselves with imagining their deaths and sad things all the time, then Jodie might have a shot here. She's been a medium for years. But would you pick up the gift if you kept feeling terrible and didn't know why? Can we at least keep it a bit more positive?"

She looked at him. "Patrick Swayze is in the room, class. The late actor. He is a good man. Welcome him and if you see him on your own turn to read, invite him to speak. He looks young. Forty, not more. He died older. That shows a strong spirit, a good mind, and a strong heart. Wish him well. He is well missed. Patrick, the world misses you." I could have burst into tears but I held it together. "You could do worse than to guide her."

CHAPTER TWENTY-ONE

June's class were responding, riveted by her. She was able to look at him and explain what she saw about him, but she was also able to bring her class back from nervousness by reflecting on his presence. The room started to feel more calm and happy again. I could tell she had led rooms for years. It was a good idea to bring us back to being a collected positive group, as well as to demonstrate her abilities. Patrick was her source for that. "Planes. A lot of planes around him. Misses flying. No, don't say anything! Not Patrick or a class member. Let's see. Jodie, do you have anything to add?'

I didn't expect that question. "About him?" I asked.

"Reading him. What do you get when you read him as a spirit?"

"I don't read him." The idea had never occurred to me. "I just talk to him," I said.

"I am understanding this," she said to herself, but aloud. "Patrick, Jodie doesn't know why you are here. No medium would unless they were used to reading the spirit and not just looking at it. This is a good thing to note class. Clearly, you are not trained, Jodie?"

I shook my head.

"Patrick says you're a natural. But you need training to understand the source of the situation. He came to you because you were one of the strongest lights in the Bay Area. To his vision, you would have been the strongest medium. He had *felt* you before his death. I say felt because I am getting this from my own guides." It was true, I could see Patrick was not speaking. "I say felt," June continued, "because he could have been in a trance or dream state or something like that. Prozac gets people there and some hallucinogens. He connected with your soul."

A hand went up in the room. "How is that possible?"

"It's possible because we have a soul." I looked at June for more information. "It can be busier than we know! We all have an aura, right? You see parts of it in pictures on those new cameras. It is way bigger than that. They cross awake and asleep. It is how some people actually meet." Patrick had a contented half smile on his face, arms still crossed. He appeared more relaxed. June continued talking to her student, a male of about twenty. "When you meet someone and you have the feeling you have always known them. Had that? That's this but he had died. The auras cross and there is recognition of work to do. It's their spirits really. In Jodie's case Patrick's spirit connected to the soul because she is fairly smart. I am sure I am right in this. He died in a sense already knowing her but not already knowing her in the way most people's conscious minds do. A yogi would know. He may have been sent by one. Jodie, can I ask you a question or two in front of the class?"

"Yes, of course," I said.

"Did you know him?"

"No. Alive? No." I can feel my heart wanting to say yes. With some urgency. "I mean, I never met him in the flesh."

"That is not what I said. Rule 101 of mystic and clairvoyant studies. The soul is bigger than the mind. You've all read it. You never met his body but in sleep states, or meditation or dreams, did he recur? Before his death I mean."

I was distracted. I needed to communicate something before I answered that question. "I need to say something," I said. "Sorry if we are derailing your class, but I have just remembered something that I think matters regarding what you just said."

"This is a class about mediumship and intuition," said June. "You have a fantastic story for us to tease out. Please, share it."

I smiled at her. "Thank you, and thank you," I said to the class. "For your patience. I believe you, June. I think I know what you mean about the spirit meeting the soul. I could feel before I came over to New York state that I was being urged. That I would get in to this course. That something was going to happen. I had an urgent inner knowing and a great sense of peace and joy about being here, that I just could not connect to a whole summer of heavy reading. I remember said to my best friend in

California that I thought I would meet my best friend in Ithaca if I didn't already have one. I just knew it from within. I told her she needn't worry because this one was male."

"Patrick. How sweet," said June. Her heart felt full of joy, her eyes were gleaming. In that second I believed. I believed that other people could benefit from me sharing this story.

It was just the greatest gift to me to be able to annunciate in this small group of people with a seventy-five-year-old practitioner exactly what I had experienced. "I believe what you are saying makes sense: he connected to my soul just a bit beyond my conscious awareness. But I knew something was going on. I didn't know it was him, but I could feel it and I was getting impressions that I discussed with people in California. Then I arrived and, bam! I know he had to get that soul awareness into my conscious waking state."

The class started clapping. Patrick grinned and took a little bow. *Off ya go, Kid.*

"My grandma helped me. She made me pick up a pendulum at first to forge the link."

June just smiled.

A hand went up. A woman asked, "What's a pendulum?"

"We use them for dowsing," said June. "And in your case. . . ?"

"Oh," I said. "I felt she was asking me to make

some letters so I could hold the pendulum over them and point to different letters to make words. I did it and she was there instantly." I couldn't help but smile. There was such joy in the sharing.

"And who is Nonny?" said June. "If I could read for you it would be with her. Patrick clearly knows how to make himself heard!"

"She is the grandma I am talking about. Everyone calls her Nonny, but Marie was her Christian name."

"We will come to her. She's a great one for you all to connect to," she told the class. "A great one for learning. We will ask her in the break. Do you think that would be ok?" she asked me.

I was touched. My grandma would have purpose and would love it. "Yes." It was hard not to cry. But we hadn't finished this conversation. It felt like one of the most important conversations of my life.

"June, what were you saying about the auras crossing?"

"Just that it likely happened even if you didn't know. That's how we meet people and think we have had past lives with them. We have met them in another state of mind. Sleeping, say. Do you remember?"

"If you would do it for me, June, I'll trade my grandma for you to read the background to that with your guides!"

The class burst out laughing. I could remember my Nonny joking about being sold in a wheelbarrow.

There was some old nursery rhyme or poem about it.

"I'll try. You'll have to connect to your heart. Close your eyes and don't say anything. And Patrick," she let out a giggle that was sweet to hear, "you shut up too! Not that you're talking. Just don't start."

"Yes ma'am." The long Texan "a" rolled like a gentle wave over the room.

I shut my eyes and searched my heart. I was interested in consciousness and it mattered that I found my truth on it. I was interested from the perspective of a scholar as well as my own heart's experience. For the sake of both, this needed sorting out. June was trying to tell me, it seemed, that it was not so random that he had shown up in Ithaca, even though she knew none of the back story. How often do we hear it—nothing is random. However it seems. I sunk into my heart and the alcoves of my mind and allowed myself a few moments.

I couldn't remember a lot of dreams, but I did get a few flashbacks. I had the definite impression that I had been fourteen when I had these supraconscious encounters. In them, he had shown me a big estate of land with hills behind it, and a red tractor. Then I had a memory of being in my mother's apartment and I could see my old bedspread. She had changed when I was twelve, so it had been before that age. He had come to my side when I was asleep, and had said, "Come on little actor, wake up again." I remembered this, but I couldn't give it an explanation at that time other than the drama competitions I had done as a child. The strongest image in my mind then came viscerally. It was when I went for an eye test and had drops in my eyes to dilate the pupils. I left the hospital so sensitive to light I could barely see to walk, and a friend had to come and walk me. I had walked outside trying to get my sense of direction for a few minutes, experiencing almost blindness from overpowering light. I shared this story about going to see the eye doctor, who had said my eyes were 20/20. I'd been having headaches and no-one could find the cause. I don't know why it seemed I had to share this story with her and the class, but I did.

Truly, I had no idea what June would say, but I felt hopeful for an explanation. Her questions had probed me into memories I had long cast aside.

June turned to her right shoulder. All mediums seem to. She spoke to her own guide and I saw him clearly. Tall, lanky and male with a good heart. He was about six-foot-four! I wanted to describe him to my tape.

"Were you at Stanford?" June asked.

"Yes!" we both said it at the same time. Patrick from the back and me from the front. Four students turned around and looked at him. He had been confident and loud.

June's guide got up and spoke again into her ear. I didn't hear it.

"Jodie, what are you doing at Cornell if you were

at Stanford? You will dislike it here! You aren't meant to be here to study. You're a West Coast girl."

"I'm just on a course for the summer. How did you know I was at Cornell?"

"Your light. It's pink at the crown. That's intelligence. And a love of it. You do the math. That's what my spirit guide says. I'd put it differently. He knows you are clever and would likely be in the area because of Cornell."

"Oh, ok. What does it matter that I go to Stanford?" I asked, unsure of where this was going.

"Is the eye doctor you went to at Stanford?" she asked, expecting a yes.

"Yes. Well, on the campus of Stanford. At the Stanford hospital." I had been back and forth on that ten-minute walk to the English department several times while they tried to solve the headache issue.

Patrick started to laugh, as he put pieces together. "Oh, God!" he chuckled.

June said, "I think Patrick might have met you there. In the way I am speaking of. At least not long before he died."

One of her student's hands shot up. "He did! I have an image in my mind like we train to in intuition class. He is walking into Stanford hospital. I can see Jodie there too, with the same kind of stone buildings, but further away. She's like a red dot on a map."

June chuckled. "That's Spirit showing you a map of the land. How far away?"

"Well she's heading that way, and there she is with the eye doctor!"

There was a real sense in the class of a forming unity. Some had only been in June's classes a week or two; others had followed her for a couple of years. Each of them was using all the training they had been given to unravel this. I was touched to experience it.

June said, "Jodie, when did you join Stanford?"

"September 2007. I visited earlier that year and then moved onto the campus for the start of the fall term."

"Was Patrick there? Yes, I think he was. There he is, walking in for treatment. Pancreatic issues." June took a step back, visibly saddened. She looked at Patrick gently. "I am so, so sorry that you passed, Patrick. It could not have been healed there. They did their best. They love you."

I felt a wave of emotion from his heart travel across the room. It was still hard to talk about death. I knew of course there was Patrick before and Patrick after. I didn't like to think of the death between and how it must have affected so many people.

"It's alright, Jodie," he said. He was heard now by a few. They told me after the class how amazed and touched they were. "You just die and then you're awake again. Don't overthink it. I'll tell you the rest of the story of getting here later."

How did he always know when I was about to cry?

"Here's an idea," said June. "How about we hear the rest of that story now?"

He laughed, emotional. "Okay!" I felt reassured he was in the room. He seemed to understand that this wasn't just a story, it was the soul of my life. So did a few of the other students. I could see it in their eyes. June was right. He did only look forty. Or around that age. The class was transfixed.

"Let's take our break," June said. "I need some orange." I'll always remember those bowls of sliced oranges. "So, geographically, you were both at Stanford. That's when this aura crossing happened for the last time, before he died." She chimed two tiny golden gongs together that were held together by a leather cord. Class was dismissed for twenty minutes.

When we reassembled, I stayed in my seat. During the break, most people had left me to myself. A couple of them had made comments like, "Patrick Swayze, wow! Such a good all round American guy." He had walked across the room, had touched my right shoulder reassuringly, and had disappeared into the other rooms of the house we were in. Mostly, the break was quiet. These students were sincere, and I could tell that each of them was preparing to bring the best of their abilities as and when they were asked to. Isn't it amazing how strangers will show up for each other when the will is good?

June played a song on her guitar to bring the class

back together. She had a sweet singing voice. She invited people to join in for the choruses, but I didn't. My heart told me to get over it and sing, but I didn't. Despite the buoyant heart, I was still a bit too reservedly English to burst into song.

"Here's what I want to do," she said. "We have a few hours left this afternoon. I would like to start this section of the class by giving Jodie a reading. Feel free to interject with your stories of Patrick Swayze if you are shown any. Invite your guides forward. But don't interrupt unless you are sure. Jodie can verify and I invite her guides to step back. There are many who will bring her to mediumship but that is not what we want now. Her mother is ill. We will send her a little blessing. And after this, if she is willing, I will invite Jodie to try a reading for one of you. Remember she has no training from what I can gather, other than what Patrick has shown her. So we will let them work together." She smiled and clapped her hands in glee. "Oh what fun!"

It's like we were back in first school, put on the spot. I was zealously excited, like when I'd been asked to read flash card words at nursery school. Patrick was rolling his nose, not liking to be put on the spot without any sense of direction or training. He'd never asked me to read a spirit. Or to read him. Or vice versa. We could hear each other and see each other and communicate at will. But I wouldn't call what we had achieved so far intuition or psychism, and neither had we experienced calling on other people who had passed over.

Well, it would be a bonding moment, if we sank or swam. "Ok!" I said, with a hopeful confidence for both of us. "We shall follow you."

"Oh, Lord!" Patrick's voice came at us as his back went the other way, to his window position. He didn't lean this time, but the arms crossed again.

"That's twice you've called the Lord in this class," I said, gently teasing him aloud. "If He's around, you might invite Him. We might need some help!"

The class tittered.

"I am doing it!" he called.

"Ok my turn. June to Jodie. First, your pendant. You saw me looking at it earlier I'm sure. The silver wing. When did you buy it?"

I didn't know if I should answer. If she was performing a reading for me, shouldn't she be making the links? But she was looking at me expectantly so I said, "I bought it for myself on a plane when I had first visited Stanford."

"You had got in and had felt the spiritual world around you, is that right?"

"Yes. I have a strong memory of that," I said.

"You will see angels. The guide wasn't Patrick. But they wanted you around. Sorry about Harvard and the other places. You needed to be where he was. It's a life plan. They are real."

It was as though she had read my applications and

the responses. I knew I had been sent to Stanford. I felt a strong sense of guidance behind me when I first walked the circular Campus Drive. Near the hospital, as it happened. I felt a guide urging me to accept the scholarship to Stanford and Stanford only. Since then, during my first year, I had started having more and more spiritual experiences, but nothing like real, conscious contact. I had seen feathers in my path so often, that I had sought out an angel reader. I had seen the rainbows and had had feathers on my right shoulder. I had seen butterflies in unusual places, and most of the other things that spiritual readers said in their books were "the signs" of being called to wake up to spirit. Until Ithaca, I had been busy with my first years of classes at Stanford, and had not been able to give these experiences much devoted time. Just a bit of internet research here and there, and a couple of visits to a famous spiritual book shop in Mountain View called East West Bookstore.

"Any questions on that?" said June.

I felt it out. "No." I just wanted her to continue.

"Your mediumship will take you places. I would like you to have the confidence to write. You can write spiritual material and be heard. The world needs it. Heaven knows we are asked by Spirit to write. Please be encouraged to pick up your pen on topics otherwise under-encouraged at Stanford. At least in your department. Which is?"

A hadn't shot up before I could answer. It was the

twenty-year-old guy. "English!" he said. "I just heard it said to my ear."

"That's right," I said. "English."

"She won't write it yet. It's going to take her ages." A middle-aged lady in the middle of the room had spoken.

June was a woman to encourage her students. I liked her for that. She wanted a calm control of the room, but didn't need the limelight. "Say more, Daphne, if you can," she said.

"I don't know why. I can just feel it. In my intuition. We won't see her writing for years. There will be another book first. And then another. About other things. Then she'll write about these days."

I noted it. Patrick and I were definitely not in the practice of prophecy, despite our many, many conversations. He told me later that he had not even fully decided that he wanted me to write a book about these Ithaca experiences yet, and he also hadn't fully considered my career as a writer of several books.

It's typical to stay fairly quiet when you are read for, and I did.

"Any more?" June asked. She was involved in her student and spoke to her guide. She told Daphne she was being congratulated on her improvement since the last time the group had met and that she would get help developing her gift further while she was sleeping and whenever she lit a candle and called good guides to her. Then she laughed, adding that her very own guide was offering to go and help Daphne.

"No," she said. "Thank you."

"There will be some trouble with this PhD. Patrick is already antsy about it. He thinks you won't finish. And I don't think he cares."

That jolted me. "I'll finish it," I said. I knew myself well enough to know that short of dropping dead, I would see the commitment out.

"I just don't feel good about it," Patrick said, shrugging.

June looked at me with some emotion in her eyes. She looked up to God. I could see the supplication. She looked at Patrick again, with some intensity.

"Patrick was not a psychic. But he feels things. The aura doesn't change a lot. I can just see that currently he is happy. He has a lot of pink in his space. Patrick, I will tell you. For many reasons, you may object to Jodie pursuing her degree in English literature. She already has one or two for sure, and that might be enough. She's a writer. You can see that. I know you see more than you know. But sort that out between you. You're a friend of sorts now. Have an opinion."

"Thank you."

"Let me finish, Dear. I am not sure quite what explains your bad feeling, but I know what explains mine. Know class that not all who serve from Spirit are trained in mediumship and prophecy. We don't just die to become a medium. It can be learned, as here. So, your guides aren't always psychics. They may have been good in business or music and can help there. Patrick is not around Jodie because he is a psychic medium who died. I do believe you will graduate Jodie, but perhaps not in the life time of your mother. I want you to go home, Dear. Not today, not tomorrow, but when you can and when you are called. Are you strong enough for this?" She looked at me kindly. Patrick opened the sliding door and walked out of the back of the house.

No. No I wasn't strong enough at all. My mother was my best friend. "Yes," I said. "I am strong enough."

"Spirit is ready for her. She's got some time. But not until you graduate."

In hindsight, I would reflect on the deep inner strength of June. On just how much it must have taken to deliver this message. The gifts of Spirit come with daily decisions, and these decisions can be powerful in other people's lives. We can, each of us, only hope that that we have made the right decision. She had, but it ripped my heart in two.

I did, in fact, lose my mother to cancer two months before I was meant to graduate from Stanford in 2013. I went back to England to spend time with her, and graduated the following year. It was a terrible loss, but June had warned me. What she did, what Nonny did, what Patrick and subsequent people I had contacted did, was train me in the tools that would help me through grief, and would hopefully help others too. It took a mature medium to predict a death in an open room of people, but she did the right thing. When the time came, I can't say I was ready—it's very hard to be truly ready to witness the death of your closest people—but I was trained. From the moment of that prediction, Patrick was relentless about me training in metaphysical understanding and practice. Nonny supported every reading I did, each one a little more confident than the last. When my mother died, I would not lose the link. They ensured it.

At that point, we were still in June's class outside Ithaca, and it was still the Summer of 2010. I had just under three years. And June called on me again to offer my first reading.

CHAPTER TWENTY-TWO

I got up and stood at the front of the room. I wished there was a chair to hold me up. All twelve students looked up at me with compassion. One middle aged lady wiped a few tears away. Patrick walked back through the door looking like he had just fallen apart and gathered himself again. They say the Divine gives you nothing you can't handle. They also say, I have learned, that the spirit world will not present you with anything that is too much. We are asked to trust both these statements. Standing there, having just heard a sudden prediction that I would lose my mother within the remaining time of my PhD course, I had to take the invitation from Spirit to face the situations in my life head on. Not later, but there and then. Via June, they had got me standing in front of a room of people who expected me to speak. I could burst into tears and flee. I could ask for a break and a breath of air. There was no use playing any "woe is me" card. There was no use complaining at the spirit world at June. I could ask for sympathy and sit down and become passive in my life and to the circumstances around me. Or I could stand and act. I could stand and be counted. I already knew it was what my mother would want me to do. She would want two things: for me to decide a life path by facing all directions available and choosing one ("we can't walk down more than one path", she would say) and, if I was going to lose her, she would want me to prepare it with as much maturity as I could.

I didn't know if Patrick already knew about my mother, but what June had suggested about him not reading people's spirits (but observing them instead), suggested to me that he had not known. But I saw instantly why he and the others who had come through on the pendulum wanted me to address and not avoid this gift while I was alone in Ithaca. I would be going home to California in a couple of weeks, and I would be sucked back into full time study and my scholarly friends again. These helpers just were not going to let that happen without me addressing this gift of mediumship, a gift I had been told I'd had for years but had ignored. I never felt that anyone on the Other Side was trying to compromise my free will—not Patrick, not Nonny, not June's tall spirit guide, and not some of the other strong characters I have been lucky enough to attract. But at the same time, they were pushing a situation that meant I had to give a reaction rather than an escape. That would help them guide me in the next steps of my life and prepare me for what would come. Patrick was never a pawn of the more experienced spirit guides like June's, who had passed long before him and had worked with mediums, but I was told that day that the sheer strength of his spirit meant he was often recruited as a messenger, and that was likely also true before his death. Others in Spirit have told me that Patrick is the ideal man among them to guide the young, the determined, or the brave and good. He didn't always have the full picture, but as soon as he'd passed over he was trusted by more advanced guides to do the right thing in a situation, which could ensure that the greater good occurred as often as possible. Given the prophecy about my mum, I knew he would think about having lost his father at a similar age. He'd been willing to let me get up there and do it thirty minutes ago, but now I knew he would help me. Neither of us were established at this. In fact, neither of us had ever given a spiritual or psychic reading before, ever. But he wasn't going to let me crash and burn. That's what Spirit noticed about him instantly. He had the heart that would step forward. They were reading him, even if he wasn't as good at reading them back. June explained this to me afterwards with a call. Sure enough, he walked through the room and came further toward my left side. Not at my shoulder, but five feet or so away.

I could see him more clearly if emotion was high. If people were sad I could see him. They say that's when visits happen. For that, or training.

I could see Patrick so clearly standing in that room. So could a few others. Well, we were going to have to get on with it. Or rather, I was.

June assured me she could help me if I needed,

and not to forget she was there. She brought me a barstool and I sat on it. I felt a bit unsteady. I did not want to feel a death again, and I wanted to have control. So, I had to take control, and establish my way. First, I had to bring a smile. I had to have a room where everyone wasn't just feeling sorry for me.

"My professors would be horrified," I said. "I am about to try to bring you knowledge out of thin air." The room chuckled.

"Saves on research time, Love," said a blonde lady from the back. She had just made herself my friend. I chuckled at that, and we were back at ease.

June brought her instruction. "Just pick someone from the class here, and then decide if you want to try contacting someone who has passed, or if you feel you want to read with the third eye to get the answer on any question they like." This caused more titters.

"That simple, then?" I asked her, wry. I wanted to ask her if she was aware that from the perspective of most people she was performing miracles every day.

"Huh? Oh, my guide says I forget." For the first time in the day she looked a little bit shy.

"I'll have a go. But just so you know, 'just pick a person and tell them the answer to anything they like' might be the most ludicrous request anyone has ever asked me!" I was teasing, and she chuckled.

"Thin air is not so thin," she said. "Off you go."

I looked at them. I didn't know the first thing about any of these women. They were all in upstate

New York and they all had name badges, but other than that they were just normal everyday people. No outlandish features, no odd dress or uniform, no *anything*, in fact, to give me any clue as to who they were or what they wanted. Nothing gave away why they, like me, had chosen to take a day to listen to a psychic medium explain her work. Their stories could be as crazy as mine.

There was one woman to the left who had a horseshoe on her sweater, so I thought maybe she liked horses and maybe she'd want to know about those. But then it could just have been her fashion statement and really she could hate animals. She blinked. Another woman by her had a big topaz ring on her wedding finger but I was sure that I had overheard her asking June for a business card to give her sister since neither of them could find a man. Maybe she was divorced. Another woman was attractive, very polished, perhaps mid-forties and well worked-out, very smartly dressed. She was wearing subtle gold at her ears, had a stiff demeanor, and looked like professional success and more success. But she was still there in that room. On a Friday. How come? This bad mental guessing was clearly not how it's done. You don't pick the answers up from how people look.

Right in front of me was a man who had said in the first toilet break that he had been practicing a lot for five years. He was now beginning to get good clarity if there was a spirit around who wanted contact. I glanced at him wondering if he would be easy since he was obviously open. As I thought it I got a quick visual impression of a black line like a crack down his front, a few inches from him. It has very dark, dense red around it. The suddenness of that threw me a bit. I wasn't ready to deal with a crack in the aura, if that was what it a professional would call it, and I backed away from opening that door. But I had at least got something. I had some information about this person that came from an additional sense. All I had done to enable it was to open to a fraction of a second of possibility, all with intent. Just that one idea that he might be easy for a beginner had given me inner hope, and instantly there had been a response of information. It was tiny, admittedly, and not something I could explain in any satisfactory way, and because of that I did not tell this man anything of what I had seen in those seconds. But still. Wow! More encouraged, I shut my eyes. I found it easier if I wasn't looking right at someone.

Right at the back of the room in front of the window was a woman who looked about forty to fifty. She had been the one with tears around her eyes after June had spoken about my mother. As soon as I closed my eyes, I had an experience like she was sending me a laser beam, or something similar. There was a sense of magnetic charge between us, and I was pulled to focus on her, eyes closed. I have since learned this practice can open the third eye in the forehead, which is the eye of the spiritual body. I suddenly felt a touch of knowing. I said to June, who was patiently reflecting the calm of the room, "I think I want to try her, if that's ok?" I must have sounded so unsure that first reading.

Make this real, I said to myself. *Make it real.*

"Sorry. . ." I said.

"Don't say sorry!" June wanted confidence. But she had a point. This was hardly taking control.

"Ok." I took a breath. "I would like to read for you," I pointed and as I heard the words coming out of my mouth, some part of me slipped from my body, turned and looked at me and shouted in my face: *Woah there! What are doing? Read for her? You're an academic!* Perhaps it was my line-towing soul. I tried to ignore it and just go with my heart. "I think rather than a question, I would like to talk to you about someone who has passed on."

She looked at me. "Okay." That's all I got.

"Right," said June, at my back. "Off you go. Tell me about the spirit."

I took the command within and repeated it with intent. *Tell her about the spirit*, I repeated a couple of times silently, willing myself. I knew there was one. My being was telling me it was right there, or actually *he* was right there. But I was not used to listening to that aspect of my being—the spirit. It was asking me to open to a whole new way of knowing, and whole new set of ears, not so much newly given but deeply buried. "I think it's a male with you." Martha just gave a non-committal nod, to acknowledge she had heard. I thought I must sound terrible at this.

A movement from Patrick caught my eye. It was just a gesture of the head, telling me to look to the back of the room.

Then I saw the man. Not clearly really, almost like an outline with some features, not all. But he was there. There really was a man standing at her right shoulder suddenly! This was the first time I had ever seen a spirit at my own calling, who had come for a total stranger. I had to stop myself from pointing or clapping myself!

June said, "What do you get on this man?"

"He's not old. He looks to be about forty to forty-five. His hair is sandy brown and totally straight, but it is longish on top and flops down a little bit over his eye. He has a jacket on and his right hand is on your shoulder, Martha." This was coming from a mixture of seeing like you see in a mirror and just knowing. This sense of knowing and having it verified was a huge opportunity, and I had to take it. Especially around Patrick. Two subtle senses were at play. I have been asked to teach this so many times, and had endeavored to bring as much detail to this first formal public reading as I can. I could not hear him saying anything. I could only see him.

Martha looked at me with caution, but she was

leaning more towards me now. She was not smiling but she was very present. I didn't get a voice from him to describe an accent, but I did find that I could almost see him better if I looked down away from him. It brought an image to my mind's eye of him standing at her back. I am wondering who this man was and figured he must be her brother since they looked the same age, or maybe a husband she had lost. I felt the emotion of that possibility. I didn't want to have to talk about a youngish death. I was not sure how I was supposed to know who he was if I couldn't hear him.

"Concentrate!" The word came with such unexpected force to the left of me that it had a physical effect. It was not June. I could feel a tingle right down the left side of me then a touch across my shoulder. As my eyes followed it I saw his hand. Pointing right at the man at Martha's shoulder. "Her dad!" then the hand retreated, as did the tingle, and out of the corner of my eye I could sense Patrick leaning against the wall to the left of me. I had been so focused on this man behind Martha that I had to tune myself to the space Patrick was in to see him. I felt a turning within my forehead, not unlike focusing a camera lens. Then I could see Patrick again. But not the other man. I wondered at this point if one was happier than the other, or if they were in different situations. The feeling of the third eye turning is a physical thing. Its opening is too. A bit like a broken heart. You can feel the pain in your chest when we are heart-broken: people clutch their chests impulsively. The third eye is the same. I could physically feel movement behind my skull, in the forehead.

I decided I was not thrown. Should I trust Patrick with this information in front of the group or not? I had seen nothing yet of this man with Martha to know his relationship with her, and I cared so much that the message was right. How did Patrick know? This all happened in about five seconds. "I know the man looks youngish, roughly the same age as you, but I think it's your father," I said. Then I didn't know where it arrived from, but following this came, as though it has just been planted in my mouth: "I think he is here to say he loves you because he died when there was tension or at least some disharmony between you, and though you have been open to contacting him before you have never managed to have contact with him." It just came straight out of my mouth. My line-towing soul watched me, amazed.

"I know he was older than this when he died, but he was miserable and he was more likely to look this way out of his own happiness at that time. I think he was a sergeant but he didn't die in that working situation." Eyes open, I got a clear visual picture in my mind of a foot and someone's hand over the top of it. This I had to translate myself. The image, the pictures and the words all came at once. I'm was trying to juggle it all to make a coherent linear sentence. It was so fast. I even started to feel a strange physical pressure in my belly that I didn't like.

I tried to piece it together. "There's a problem with his foot I think. Wait! Is that you, since it looks like a female foot? Ow!" I had just shouted in pain. "Sorry, I've just got this feeling. Did he pass or get ill with something to do with his bowel or intestines?" I was hurting there right now, and I'd never experienced this before. It was not searing pain, but just a funny feeling of discomfort, different from suddenly having gas or indigestion.

June put her hand on me. "Ok, now let her respond." Everyone in the room was either staring at me or turning around to look at her. I didn't know if I was right. Doubt was crushing my chest, fighting, but something was fighting back. Martha looked right at me, right into my eyes. "Does he say why we weren't friends?"

I wasn't sure what I do, but I did what felt right and looked to her shoulder. No voice came, just an intuition.

"Did he desert you?" That was the word. Not leave, or abandon, or walk out. Desert. As soon as I said it I wanted to take it back. The desire for the knowledge, to get her what she wanted, had meant I hadn't quite processed the information emotionally before I had passed it on. It was a lesson for me. If I weren't reading excitedly I wouldn't put it that way, so starkly. Once I had said it, I knew that if it were true, it must have been a sore wound for Martha. My own father left when I was seven, suddenly. I wanted to go to Martha and give her a hug and say I was sorry. You can't do that with a professional reading. I knew it from the way June's hand had not moved from my shoulder. I learned then and there that in the moment my job was not have the emotional response that would get in the way of telling her what the spirit world was trying to say. My job was messenger, and my own soul could decide just how to put the message, but not change it or pity it.

Martha just started to cry. *Oh no.* On instinct, I looked for Patrick. He was there, watching. He said to me, quietly, "You've got to handle it."

The only thing I could do was think about what I would want in Martha's situation. It was so real and emotional. Martha was vulnerable and now I felt I owed her something.

"Shall I carry on?" I asked her as tenderly as I could.

June said, firmly, "Yes!" Martha looked at me, screwing up tissues, and nodded yes.

"Is this making any sense to you?" I asked.

"Yes," she said. "I'm sorry, carry on. He died with bowel complaints." That made me nervous. I turned to June, nearly losing it.

"Should I be able to feel that in my own body?" I asked her. This was twice now. I was nervous about sharing my growing mediumship with other people if I was going to keep feeling these physical sensations.

"It's one way information comes," June says. "If you pursue this you can ask Spirit to change your connection. Perhaps you were once a shaman healer."

"I'm a student."

"Not in this life, Dear."

Oh. A few people giggled at me.

"Should I continue for you if you are not comfortable?" June asked. "I would like you to complete if you can, but I can take over." I looked for Patrick. He held one finger up. I had no idea what that meant. I wanted to get it right.

"I think I'll just try once more, if I can," I said. Everyone nodded. I looked at her and had to really still myself. I had to take those moments to get out of my head and my emotions and let the connection happen again. This receptive state is not a natural state for most people. It had not been for me. I realized I was always, always thinking or feeling. To get anything from Spirit, I had to be so present in that moment, oblivious to everything else, perhaps like a soccer pro as he is standing about to take a make-or-break penalty. I saw the father again and he was looking at me, but I couldn't hold him. He kept slipping in and out of my vision. I had to shut my eyes and breathe. Be still. Then, connected again, I just knew what he was pushing on me, this father. "There is a letter unopened, you have to see it and then he'll be at peace."

June said: "Good. I believe you are right there."

Martha said, in the same instant, "Where?"

I looked at him and I couldn't see him anymore. I didn't get anything. *Damn!* I asked in my mind about the letter. Nothing came to me. But I just have an urge, from somewhere else. I was told this information from a source other than the father, and behind me. I repeated it. "It's in a document carrier in a box, overlooked."

Martha was shaking her head.

"And for some reason I don't think it is from him," I said. "The letter was written by someone else."

She looked up at me. "I'll find it," she said, with some certainly. "That made sense."

I couldn't believe all this had come from me. "Thank you," I said. I had had enough. "I think that's all I can get," I said. I got up and went back to my place on the sofa and sat down. Patrick, right by my chair, gave thumbs up. I was kinda proud of that, as he might say. *Way to go, Kid.*

Wow.

The ladies in the room started clapping for me. The nerves drained and my heart opened a little. "Thank you."

For the rest of the day, two more people tried to do their own readings, and June made sure each of us had received a message from Spirit. I was overjoyed to watch and to think that all this time in Ithaca would come to good for more than me. Perhaps I would have a chance to make the world a better place.

Perhaps a more hopeful place. Perhaps Patrick would be a part of that. I was thrilled at the prospect of sharing his goodness with other people, so that he could potentially continue his positive impact on the world from across the so-called divide.

CHAPTER TWENTY-THREE

Edward called and I shared the day. I tried to push out a dreadful feeling that I was about to lose my marriage. "It's not a total surprise, is it?" I asked. "Remember that voodoo woman in New Orleans with all that crazy stuff on the walls who said she knew your life from looking at chicken bones?" We had been to her on account of all the words in that last sentence. We'd been so intellectually intrigued when we had walked past her building and had seen her sign outside, that we just had to try it.

Edward laughed lightly. I know we were both remembering a day in sheet rain at the edge of the French Quarter before the disaster that hit New Orleans. We had danced with two old men playing the saxophone who had a checkers board. We got totally soaked with them in the rain, laughing and feeling free. Then we'd sheltered from the weather by going to see this lady for half an hour. She had eyes that said several people lived behind them—piercing and wild. She grabbed a velvet bag full of dead chicken bones and threw them out onto an open table. She had just looked at them, bits of foot bone and rib, maybe some beak, and had started talking.

"She did know we worked with books!" Edward said. "From that bit of gristle." I had met him during our interview period to work at the same publisher in

London.

"She also stabbed at her forehead with her own fingernail and told me I was a seer." I said. "Do you remember that?"

"That was some holy chicken!" said Edward, wry as always.

She'd talked for a while actually, in a thick accent I could barely understand. "I ignored everything in that reading," I said, "because she said ultimately you would just be my friend."

We hadn't been married then, but I knew we would be. I felt happy calling the memory back. We had followed that reading with gumbo in the rain and a vodka drink with an unexpected oyster at the bottom of the glass. Edward had brought his straight back up, almost all over the table. We had travelled the States together as friends. We both loved New Orleans, with its huge soulful singers who laughed from deep within, its iron ornate balconies, gumbo, juleps and feathers, and charismatic faces with teeth missing, deep lines and lots of character. People there had stories. The town was a playground with the right sensibility for us: a little moody, a little spirited, anti-Vegas, which was not our thing. We'd played in Vegas on our road trip, but it wasn't a place to catch your heart. "The only thing I can remember from that voodoo woman," I said, "apart from all that, is that we had to drink more and dance more together. Let our hair down to bond."

"Now that is still true." Edward was very good at

both drinking and dancing, when he took the time. I couldn't do either very well, and I certainly needed the first to dare attempt the second.

"See? So, it is possible! That she knew things." I was going to try to win this; I had my in. "And remember Sweetheart that once in your life you have been to see a medium."

"So?" he said. "I was curious. It doesn't mean I am into mediums. I seem to remember *someone* is always advocating an open mind."

"I am. And did she make it all up, all that stuff the medium said about you?"

"You know she didn't," he says. I could hear the sigh in his tone and the plea in mine. I couldn't help it.

"Not bonkers then?" God, he was making me work for it.

"Yes, totally bonkers! This information coming from nowhere is totally bonkers. It's totally mad! Like my wife, apparently."

Ah. That was problem. *Like his wife.* I told myself his heroes were all off-the-wall mad people and geniuses. Leonardo da Vinci. Jorge Luis Borges. Herman Hesse. Philip K Dick. He would not leave me for mad.

"But not quite so cute as me," I said.

"No, Darling. Not as cute."

I could hear the strain we were both trying to patch. My heart was stretching to the point of a tear. I think his was, too.

"I have to go now. I'll do some reading."

"Have a vino with your Derrida anthology," he said. "And come home soon."

"I love you," I replied, and hung up.

Patrick had not heard this conversation. When I heard his voice an hour or so later, it was bouncy.

"Well you deserve a glass of wine!" It seemed everyone was advocating wine.

"Thank you," I said aloud, not looking for him.

"What's the problem?" he said.

"What if I don't know who I am anymore?" I was surprised just how flat my voice sounded.

"What do you mean? You did great!"

"My experiences."

"Are great! Well done!"

He walked to the fridge. Opened it. Reached for wine. I literally saw him open it and take the wine. And yet physically, my fridge door was closed. Plato wrote about things taking form on different levels, different dimensions. So had Heidegger, but he had stated it differently. I was so flat in mood, I barely reacted. But as clear as I could see my own hands, I saw him Patrick do this. It was as though we lived in two worlds, and by "we" I meant the living and the dead, and they were almost exactly the same and yet a million miles away too. He was pouring wine, sniffing it, sipping it, spitting it into the sink in elaborate jest. Fair enough; it was about seven bucks. I wondered how much a bottle of vino cost in glory days of Tinsel Town. I felt calm and numb, and just watched these gestures. I was still enough to notice that the center of my forehead was active, as well as my eyes, in seeing him. When I turned that inner eye downwards, which felt like a movement under my skin, I couldn't see him. I just saw my fridge, still closed. I played with it silently for a few moments. Inner eye up: I saw him. Inner eye down: he had gone. I had of course heard this phrase "opening the third eye". Now I realized this was a very literal opening. It wasn't idiom. I could feel it under my skin. Was it part of the brain, or part of what some mystics have called the subtle bodies, meaning the bodies of lighter frequency that leave the physical body after death and sometimes travel during sleep and near-death experience?

Patrick wasn't doing physical things. He was moving some sort of astral or quantum element of them. I was aware of the magnitude of what I was seeing, but I had no framework to explain it, and my sadness about my tension with Edward kept me still.

"This is awful wine," Patrick said. "You should upgrade."

He was right. It was awful. But it was all I thought I could afford.

I felt like I would break his heart if I told him how I was feeling. He looked anxiety free and it was a beautiful thing. But we were getting off line here, two parallel tracks veering quickly in different directions.

The train would break apart if I didn't speak.

"These experiences. . ."

"Are great. I keep telling you!"

"Patrick. My experiences are not in line with my identity. I don't doubt that they are real. I just have too many gaps. Too many bridges to cross mentally. My husband is not taking this easily. Some other people likely won't. People I care about."

"Why not? Am I going to have to prove myself forever?" He seemed fractious, but calm enough.

"No, but you could tell me a few things. Like how did you find me in Ithaca? Is it true that we had a link from the time you were at Stanford hospital?"

"I don't know," he said. "I don't know all that stuff about the soul. You need a guru for that. It's possible. I can feel truths and responses inside me that I can't always vocalize. Always had them."

"So, what do you know? How come you were just in this apartment in Ithaca?"

"You don't know?" he asked. "I presumed you did." He stumbled a bit, remembering. He smiled. "I guess I always thought you could see. Even in East West. It seemed that way."

"East West Bookstore in Mountain View?"

"Yes! Jodie, I got to Ithaca because I followed you."

For some reason that stunned me more than if he has said he had arrived in a golden space ship. But I supposed it was more rational. "From where?" I said.

"Jodie, I have been guiding you since I died. I followed you because I had to get you into a place alone so you could come to choose between two directions in your life. Your other guides call it an intervention."

"What's an intervention?"

"It's when spirit is seen. They cross to guide something or to force something, or to enlighten on something. I suppose that's me now. You need to be making some major life decisions and we are here to help you."

"That's why I was used to feeling you around! At home, I mean. I didn't know it was you, but I felt someone around in Mountain View."

"I know, I saw you tell Edward. I knew you had the light on for mediumship or I wouldn't have tried. I saw others in East West. I followed you there."

I had been to the metaphysical book shop several times since I went to Stanford. Once I walked the seven miles there and back, following an inner pull to be there. I was searching for something there, and kept coming home, of course, with more books.

"Wow," I said. I felt the acceptance inside of me. I had given him a hard time. It wasn't his fault or his privilege that I was a medium. I had been told I had been for a very long time. But it was definitely to his credit that I had accepted it, and if I could serve with it that would be to his credit, too. And to Nonny's. I decided then and there that I would not give him or this gift a hard time again. When you have been given a gift from God, it's rude to whine.

CHAPTER TWENTY-FOUR

I was in a dream, but I hadn't not yet realized it. I was in Cambridge, walking through where I lived in my first year as an undergraduate student. I guess I was revisiting, tracing old ground to help me decide what would come next. I had been very happy at Cambridge. The Cripps buildings at the back of St. John's was where I first felt I truly belonged after my first boyfriend had broken my heart. I felt cradled by Cambridge, intellectually and spiritually. I recognized at the time that St. John's would always be one of my favorite places on Earth. When I did my Masters in Metaphysical Science come years after this dream, I learned the attitudes towards dream from the perspective of spiritual and metaphysical teaching. It's because of that training that I've included two prominent dreams I had in Ithaca here. At St. John's, Patrick was walking along beside me. I showed him my old room from the outside —D6. His arm round was thrown around me casually, as you might walk with your close friend. In hindsight, it might also be how someone would hold you if they were trying to guide you. He had a certain steering power with his arm cast over my shoulders like that. Here we were looking at the time I fell in love with being in a university setting. Patrick looked young and so did I, though slightly older, I now realize, than I was when I was last there.

In spiritual language, that would mean my astral body was developing. It wasn't as old as my physical body, meaning I hadn't done a lot of spiritual research yet. Now when I dream and look in a mirror, I am about the same age as I look in physical life. There is so much to learn about the so-called subtle bodies—and at that time I still had so much to learn. But I had started to think about it, and in that I had started to notice things like my apparent outward age in dreams, or Patrick's apparent outward age when I could see him.

We walked under an ivy-covered Victorian arch onto a building they used to nickname the "architectural typewriter". This was the 1960s Cripps Building: the college has quads from different eras of architecture as the college has expanded since it was founded in the fifteenth century. Cripps was hideous to me then, but then I was a philistine, and so was Patrick who said: "Where the hell are we?"

"Here!" I walked around the court with him to the right of me. And then I started to feel lucid. I knew consciously that I was in a dream and that my body was sleeping in bed. I know I didn't have to wake it up and that I could walk around here while my body slept peacefully. I suppose most people would call it lucid dreaming.

I walked him into the building we used to have plays in, and some big college parties, and music practice rooms. It is called the Fisher Building, and is very modern compared to the history there. I was talking to Patrick and above all things I felt safe. Patrick was wearing a tank top. I don't know why. I just felt lucidly that I must have brought him here for a reason. I turned to him in the flow of our conversation about the college and my fun memories there—I think I was asking permission to stay with university life—and I put my hand on his shoulder.

Instantly something fired in my brain that this was not normal. Or at least it was not normal to the percentage of my brain that I had been using up to that point in my life. *I am dreaming,* I told myself. *Lucid Dreaming.* But something is off. I could feel my spirit telling me rapidly with urgency that I needed to record this. I had to use will, strong will to remember it when I woke up. So many people, my spirit told me, lucid dream and forget. It just takes will to remember. To not block it out from childhood training to not see more than this supposed, culturally trained "what is".

Here is what was off. *I could feel skin.* I felt a recognition that typically when I am dreaming I don't feel skin. I put my hand on Patrick's shoulder again. It felt exactly like the skin on a newborn's leg or on the very inside of a woman's arm, incredibly soft. My mind was stirring. I knew this was metaphysically important and would be important to mediums, but I couldn't balance my emotions well enough to think clearly in that lucid moment. I mean, skin! On a dead person! I couldn't get my emotions to calm from that experience. Neither of us was "in body" but both of us still had skin! My emotions were so excited that at that time my mind couldn't discipline them to experience this more fully. It would take a lot of meditation before I had that control in lucid dreams.

I felt I was slipping from Patrick, about to fall back into my sleeping body. He reached and touched me gently on the chin. I felt it, the real touch of a finger. I was stunned. Too stunned to explain what my mind was trying to process about unspoken or undiscovered research on the afterlife. I knew then for sure that this research area was vast. I wanted every superior mind in the world on the case. I knew it mattered. To more than faith—to history, to science, to all the world's disciplines. But I was too stunned to keep my calm and stay in that dream. I was pulled up through what felt like a tunnel and it seemed for a second that I was coming around from a deep anesthetic, groggy and reluctant. Then I was in my bed, waking, eyes still closed. This touch, I knew, had been real. It was of more than mind: there was a dimension. Skin. Somewhere. Where was that somewhere? Do we all go somewhere else at night?

Again, I had been shown something I knew but don't want to have to face in my life: the difference between what *is* and what can be explained. Did I just let it go or pursue it? I felt if I pursued it, this research would always be part of my life for as long as I lived. *Skin.* I lay in my bed and thought about it. Patrick was still there somewhere. He really was. So, therefore, were hundreds of other people who had died. I had yet to witness this of course, but it became so clear to me that I had to confront this and speak about the afterlife, even if it threatened my relationships or position at Stanford. This wasn't religious, as talk about the afterlife is often taken to be. It was surely scientific. I just didn't know of the tools in the material plane that could adequately research the non-material planes. On top of that, I had just experienced them for the first time (and not the last), that there was still physicality. I didn't have the scientific training, but I knew someone somewhere did, and would make the link between my experience and quantum physics. I woke with that phrase in my mind. *Quantum mechanics* was the phrase I wrote in my journal, having never heard much if anything about it. String theory. Then I put a line through that phrase, and wrote, QUANTUM. It was a message. I just didn't have the quantum theory training. Then I wrote, also in capital letters. IT WILL EXPLAIN IT. JUST SHARE. I couldn't do all the research myself. Patrick was not just a memory for someone, or a vibration, or an energy. He was still someone formed. I thought they might all be, those people we have lost. Cruelly close, it felt sometimes. But not gone. Still active, doing something somewhere in the universe. I lay there in bed and felt more hope for this world than I ever had before.

Three days later I had another lucid dream in which Patrick took me to meet his wife Lisa. We were at some sort of venue for a show, waiting for a music gig. The area was fairly small and indoors, perhaps for a thousand people. Patrick was standing on the stage, wearing a cowboy hat. He looked somewhere around fifty years old, or a little younger. Later in my notes I wrote that he may have been wearing some sort of glasses, or else he had been doing at that time, or that day. He had a laminated pass round his neck. He came to give me one. It clearly said VIP. I'll remember thinking *Ah, this is how you live, and this is how I live.* In the dream, I knew he was famous and that somehow I knew him. I wondered if this was in the past. Maybe I was revisiting a scene in his life with him, as I had taken him back to Cambridge.

A blonde lady approached, beautiful with very long hair, which was very straight, almost ironed-looking. I knew she was Lisa but also I knew I had not met her before. Patrick took me to her and said, "Lisa, Baby, this is my friend. Her name is Jodie."

Lisa smiled and said, "Oh hi!" She seemed a little surprised I think, that he had just manifested a friend in an almost empty room. But she was accepting enough, waiting for the concert and distracted by the waiting. She was a wearing brown suede jacket with blue jeans. She looked younger than she must have been. Good bones. Patrick had married a beautiful, friendly woman and I felt pleased and relieved about it.

Soon the room was full and a band was playing. The pair of them were surrounded by friends at the front of a full crowd, both sociable and laughing. They looked to be enjoying themselves and each other. He kept his eye on me, brought me a bottle of beer held high above the heads, but mostly he lets me be and went to enjoy his time there. I was not standing with them.

When I woke, I wondered if this was a return favor from his soul. Maybe this time he took to somewhere when he had been really happy, just as I had shown him the college where I felt joyful and like I belonged. What mattered beyond that was this ongoing expansion of communication in waking and sleeping states. We were preparing the way for other people who had passed to make contact with me awake and asleep and in as many ways as possible. Through mind, through image, through the spoken word, through the gentle intention of telepathy, what we were achieving was the rapidly opening of my mental and spiritual capacities. At that time, I was not meditating, which is the one tool that enables the opening of the mind for giving and receiving far beyond our everyday conscious capacity. But I was sleeping deeply and practicing everything we could think of in as many settings as possible. We tried to communicate inside, outside, in public settings and where there was no-one to focus on the other one. That way we could limit distraction and enable focus.

In the years that have passed I have been incredibly grateful for this start because it meant that I wasn't one track in my ability to receive from the spirit world. I was able to help other people with it very quickly.

What was still limited was my ability to read deeper into the spirit and the soul. After a week or so of further dedicated training with Patrick, I could pick up intended communication in lots of ways. I got a few headaches and sometimes light nausea. I wasn't worried about it: it felt like some internal pathways were shifting. I was pleased with it: delighted with the progress. I could speak to Patrick—and presumably any other spirit I'd have future contact with—without having to move my lips. That meant I could achieve communication in public without having to move my lips and look crazy to living people who had not yet opened their third eyes to see. Of course, June's prediction about my mother's death was one motivation in my heart, but it wasn't one I shared with anyone. I was very close to my mother and feared her death tremendously. I had already lost both my grandmothers very recently. Even as a growing medium, I feared her death. I feared the dying part, what I would see her go through most of all. She had a blood disease that we had held off over several years by listening to her doctors and to many holistic healers. The fear was that it would turn into cancer of the blood. I had no idea what such a death would be like for her, and I was so scared of her going through it that I focused on developing mediumship with all the inner peace that lived inside me. I didn't have any developed healing ability, although I knew these powers with Spirit could link to the ability to bring some forms of healing. It was my personality to approach the prediction of my mother's death by first developing mediumship since that was what happened to be in front of me, on offer from Patrick. Then, later, I would try to learn to heal. At least if medicine and spiritual efforts failed, I would be able to speak to her.

Patrick protected me with a fairly stern reticence when it came to speaking about his own cancer and death. I believe he'd made the decision to focus on the positive as much as possible. He told me things often like he was no longer in pain, and that the drugs help, and that doctors are good, and that science is developing. I knew he remembered deep physical pain since I saw him wince a few times when I asked, and I knew it was in memory. He was not interested in spreading fear. Patrick was worried about cancer in general as a Western killer. I could feel he carried a sort of mental malaise regarding cancer (not a mental illness at all, but a feeling of sickness when he thought about it), and that sickness was not about his own suffering with it, but how thousands and thousands are still suffering. He wanted it addressed. He didn't talk about it much at that stage, but I knew the suffering of so many people was a burden he felt deeply for the world. I feared the loss of my mother acutely and I believe he worried about it for me. Not wanting to make the worries of each other worse, we didn't speak about it a lot. We did the best we could with communication techniques, and Nonny complimented that with communication using tools. I kept using the pendulum to talk to her, and I thought about what the source of the movement of that stone on a chain could be. She had been interested in divination and prediction in her own life, and it was clear that those topics remained of interest to her. The two of them approached me differently and naturally started to develop different skills of psychic mediumship with me. My Nonny ultimately wanted to make a psychic of me. Patrick wanted to make the medium. He would ensure that if the prediction of my mother's death was to come true, I would know her from Heaven. His commitment to help someone he had never known staggered me. It was humbling to witness first hand that his global fame had ruined nothing in him that is precious in humanity.

If his fans could know and take from this memoir just that fact, I would be happy.

CHAPTER TWENTY-FIVE

It was the birthday party of one of the girls in our class. Twelve of us had been invited to join a dinner in a restaurant downtown, followed by cake and games in a big shared student house. I was happy to be going out. I called a hiatus for a day on researching mediumship after my obligatory hour and a half of reading for class. I had a bath, did my hair, got made up. I put a black dress and heels on. I would have to manage them on the Ithaca slopes. I hadn't bothered much with my appearance for a few weeks.

I heard a whistle as I left the apartment. I stopped me in my tracks and I turned.

"Well. Don't you look mesmerizing."

Gee thanks, Patrick Swayze! "Oh."

"Have fun," he said. "Don't be back late."

"Ok, Dad."

There was a chuckle. "I'm going to read the pages for your dissertation on the desk there."

"Enjoy." I picked up my bag and opened the door.

"Jodie?"

"Yes."

"Don't get too drunk, now."

"Ok, Dad." I turned back around, feeling sassy. "Patrick?"

"Yes?"

"I am twenty-nine. That is nearly thirty."

"Yes. Just old enough to be my daughter."
This paternal side of him was nice.
"I'll be home my midnight," I said.
"Eleven. Thirty."
I chuckled.
It's a funny thing, life. They say it's a gift. Believe them.

I had a good time. We overate and over drank. I did not get "too drunk". But we did play charades and other silly games until way after eleven thirty. The next morning wasn't pleasant. I was one of approximately all of us who did not want to go to class. But I got up to go. I stood at the stove waiting for a pan of water to boil for morning tea. I thought I better also boil a couple of eggs.

"You need to get divorced." Patrick wasn't usually there talking in the mornings, but this was a change. Perhaps he was checking if I was still functioning after a few gin and tonics.

"Huh?" Where had that come from? He stated it like a bold, bald fact. He was standing by the window.

"I'm sorry. I, I just. It's not my business. But I also care. And we need to talk about this. We do. Can we talk about this? Hello Jodie?"

"Um. . ."

"Jodie, can we talk about your marriage?"

In my notes from that day I had written that he went from bold and firm to apologetic and shy about the topic in a matter of seconds. I have written that he was questioning himself on the appropriateness of his comment if I were his medium, and then that he came forward with it again, more confident that it was appropriate, because he perhaps saw me as his friend.

What did I feel in response to that surprise comment? Nervous, I think. He was about to rip the lid off another can. This time of worms.

"Of course," I said. I sat down on the sofa.

He laughed. "You're so English."

What could I say to that?

He moved from the window to next to the sofa but he remained standing. I could see him clearly and in full color. The shirt was blue.

"Jodie, I don't think you're going to be happy and I feel it's my duty to tell you. I feel like a parent to you some days. That's a funny thing about care and friendship, isn't it? You change all the roles around."

"I understand," I said.

"Okay."

That was all that was said about it.

Later, I was lying on my bed reading and I felt a tug at my right foot. Very, very slowly, I was pulled backwards off my bed and onto the floor. I didn't resist, but I didn't aid him with one muscle.

On the floor, I turned over of my own volition. That had capped it as the strangest experience of my life to date. Though he didn't quite manage it, I could feel the effort to pull me up. I stood, alone in the room to any non-clairvoyant eye, but for fresh air. I let my body go limp, standing upright in a pair of leggings and a T-shirt. Again, I started to move, not of my own volition. Inch by inch I was bent backwards from the waist, as though there were a forearm at my back supporting my weight. I was leaning back over it. My feet stayed on the floor but I was folded almost in two, pushed inches further than my muscles were happy with. I could feel my abdominals start to quiver in resistance but I didn't fall. I was being held, my eyes on the back wall now, moving slowly, hair touching the floor. I could feel the pull at my hip flexors and grimaced.

"I am not a dancer!"

"Shame. But don't tell me there are no miracles. Never again."

I was straightened, gracefully. I would have fallen without support. I knew I could not bend like that on my own. It was as though he had simply forgotten he was not physical any more, or has willed it not to be the case. In whatever reality that is, the strength of his will was moving mountains.

My strongest ability at that stage was hearing, or clairaudience. I could hear real voices most of the time, and sometimes a sort of telepathic transmission into my own mind. I got sentences that were not my own but without particular tone or accent. I had learned to tune in to Patrick's voice by meditating with it and by allowing it to flood into my mind. The power of will, or the power of gentle but continuous intent, really did work. Without question, my abilities got better with practice. Good intention helped, and calm. Positivity in general opened more doors. My fearful days were when there was some snapping between Patrick and I as I tried to learn more, and on the same days I snapped a bit at Edward. Positivity is expansive—it brings new experience and opportunity in all areas of life. It is just the same with trying to contact the spirit world. I thought about Nonny doing Ouija during the Second World War with other wives at home. I hadn't thought about it for a while, but she had told me about it when I was in my early teens. Every weekend she and her friends on her street would listen to air raids, not knowing whether their husbands had lived or died that day. Nonny and her sister had hosted séances where they had asked the spirit world to tell them. She told me that they got accurate information from that glass, which was eventually confirmed by news reports and letters home.

I know there is a lot of fear in our culture about Ouija, and that Hollywood hasn't done much to deconstruct the fear and hysteria that surrounds it. I had some fear about sharing the truth about my use of the pendulum with other people, because of the stories about Ouija. My experiences have only ever been positive and verified. Nonny's were in the war. Having had some time since practicing contacting the heavens, I really believe that intention, will and positivity are the keys for an appropriate experience, even if that experience is an apparent non-response.

I had another memory about doing a Ouija board with my Nonny present when I was in my early teens. Again, I hadn't thought about it for a long time, but when I think about spirit contact I can remember it vividly. I had felt great lightness flow through me when I first touched a glass on an upturned table. Over the course of the first ten minutes we had got random letters. There were about eight fingers on the glass. Nothing made sense. The glass kept moving towards me and stopping still. Of course, there were some with too vivid imaginations in the room. Did it mean I was about to die? Did it mean the message was for me? Perhaps because I had seen some spirits as a little girl, I didn't feel the drama, but I also wasn't able to silence it in the room. The atmosphere became about intrigue and excitement mixed with fear, rather than loving respect for the concept of a benevolent Heaven and a Source—call it God, Source, Universe, that might be more knowing than us and benevolent too.

Before long, the glass was moving erratically around a large dining table, and with an energy that told me it might smash. Finally, the letters spelled that one of the people present had to leave the room. They were scared and felt rejected, but they had been disrespectful, provoking fear, shouting about evil spirits unnecessarily. That person left and the glass gently brought a message from Nonny's sister and then from the father of someone else who was present. I watched with a real inner calm. As I reflect on that calm now, it is perhaps no wonder I was to become a medium. I could see the same dramas on offer from some planes of the Other Side, just as we are offered silly dramas on Earth. It was quite clear that we were reaping what we sowed.

Eventually, the glass pointed that only my finger should be on the glass. The table agreed, and the glass spelled out simply, Bless You. I asked it gently what we might all do in that moment, with this situation of contact. It moved smoothly, with peace. Go to sleep now all, it said. And be good to Heaven.

I don't think I did the Ouija board again after that. Some people my age decided to play with it the following week with just that intent—play. I declined to attend. I knew the hearts going to call in spirit were going for the wrong reasons. They wanted to be scared, or to impress the girls, or to stir something up. That's what they got. They told me they tried again the next week, this time much more clearly to impress a new girl in the town. The glass didn't move. They reported all of this to me, I think to try to rile me because I'd been chosen to have my finger on the glass. I didn't say a lot. What is there to say? *Go figure.*

I believe it's possible to have a good relationship

with the spirit world, whether we see those dimensions or not, and that each of us can feel if our relationship is good in our hearts. I didn't practice Ouija, but I had approached it with love, respect and peace. I had seen a couple of psychic mediums in my life before I moved to California, and while I didn't understand where their information was coming from (accurate that it was), I was open to listening, respectful, and was unafraid. I made sure that I paid the psychic mediums for their time, and that I verbally told them I appreciated their gift in the world. I noted their advice in my journals of the time, and I followed it the best I could. When I was blocked by my own worry, I said so whenever I felt a presence around me.

I can't tell you for sure why I had this wonderful experience with my grandma when I picked up a pendulum in Ithaca, or why a kind movie star was willing to stick around and give me some training, but, again, go figure. I believe in treating well those things we can't necessarily see. I believe in respecting the information of the sages that has been passed down through oral, artistic, spiritual and literary traditions. While I hadn't much pursued mediumship or the metaphysical, other than some attempts with a tarot deck and happy, curious conversations with any mystically inclined person I met, looking back I did consciously maintain a good and respectful relationship with the spirit world that I thought might really be out there. I was rewarded for that, and I made sure my gratitude was known.

My abilities grew rapidly in Ithaca. I had been guided to three mediums in a short time, and I reflected on their approaches and all they had said. I tried to find my own boundaries and parameters and, without a professional teacher, I did the best I could with the pendulum, with reading bits of Sylvia Browne, and with asking Patrick to practice with me. My personal essay writing gave way to writing my daily notes, but I was happy to be making progress.

Seeing was secondary to hearing for me, but it was developing the more I practiced. We did lots of exercises around seeing. "How many fingers am I holding up?" became asking me to see how many fingers with my eyes closed. I found my vision with my eyes closed was almost 360 degrees, and with some googling read that such vision is normal in the subtle bodies if not the physical body.

We also investigated whether I could see an idea in Patrick's mind more and more, and I especially remember an evening where I asked him about events in his life and asked him to see if he could show me in images. I knew some mediums described images that were put into their minds for their clients. I got fairly good at that. I went to bed with a throbbing forehead some evenings. More googling about mediumship told me that these aches were apparently quite normal as we link the mental to the metaphysical and spiritual aspects of man.

I had always been good at sensing presence. That, I learned, is our conscious awareness picking up on the frequencies touching our spirit, just as our physical body might tell our conscious awareness when it is picking up the frequencies of a hot sun. Now I could focus on that sense of presence or contact for the person to reveal themselves. Mostly of course this had been Patrick. He had been the one most willing to step forward and help me to bring spiritual capacities to my conscious awareness. But now I had seen these other people in the street just as clearly.

Naturally I was interested in the experiences of other people and whether most of them believed mediumship was a gift or whether it could be taught. The books I had bought in Ithaca on the topic suggested that mediumship is a gift that tends to run down a family line: some people have it and some don't. But I also found courses online claiming to be able teach mediumship to people with no previous sense of a gift. My own opinion at that time could only come from my own experience. Yes, from a young age I had some sort of sensitivity, but I had also chosen in these last weeks to spend considerable time focusing on it and developing it. My attitude was that this gift could likely be developed in the very willing, if not quite taught in a theoretical class. By that, I believed the skills needed to be routinely practiced, just as an athlete would need to keep their body in training. To me, to say the gifts of mediumship are only available to a few is to deny that each and every one of us has a spirit with some potential.

I was aware from looking in metaphysical book shops of channeling, which had seemed to have a big vogue in the 1960s. I had read about Edgar Cayce and other such people who had written many books as so-called trance-channels. They had essentially loaned their physical selves to the spirits that had passed who claimed to be their higher guides. They had been conduits in that way to bring forward whole book shelves of information.

I asked Patrick his opinion on channeling.

"What exactly do you mean?" he asked.

"Channeling is where you let someone else talk right through you."

'Should they need permission?" he asked.

"Of course. On both sides. Everything has to be ethical."

"I think there are people in California north and south who don't practice those ethics. It's important you tell them. People have been calling me with Ouija boards and tarot and every tool and medium they can find since 2009, almost before I had even died. I could feel it and my spirit guide confirmed it when I crossed. You'll never be blamed for that. I came to you. But I was slowed down by incessant calls from your side to mine: *'Patrick come and see us! Come show yourself!'* I was amazed June picked me up. I usually stay away. I want you to tell every medium or channeling junkie you meet to practice really strong ethics and to teach them to the world. Not for fear, but so that good is done all round."

"Ok," I said. "I am sorry you have been through any of that."

"I didn't know channeling was a big thing. I hadn't heard a lot about it."

"It's a New Age thing that people got into for the wrong reasons after Edgar Cayce. People talk about them in the metaphysical book shops and hippie type of shops. I have seen it here and in LA and all over. Mostly it's not for real and good research and, hey, if you're not a medium it's not strictly necessary, is it."

What Patrick has said about channeling satisfied some of my curiosity and hit some of my subconscious fears about it. I was worried that this might just happen to me, or that I would be approached by someone who had died who was not coming from the good. I didn't know much and felt these worries were natural. They were either my mind and emotions playing tricks with my ignorance, or perhaps this was something that might happen to me. I'd found an area of metaphysics that I felt quite scared of when I thought about it. I knew other people had written books reporting positive and wonderful experiences with their guides from channeling, but somewhere in my subconscious I was worried about it.

I was quiet for about a day before I explained this to Patrick. Perhaps I sounded suddenly like a nervous little girl, scared of what might be out there that I couldn't quite see yet.

"Ok," he said. He sounded old and wise in that moment. "Sit there."

"Why?" I said, sitting.

"I'll show you."

I just sat there. I trusted him more than anyone else in this situation.

He walked across the room and sat down on the same kitchen chair I was sitting on.

I could not feel him at all.

"Be passive," he said. "I knew you'd ask about this in the end, Miss Research Material, so I did some asking yesterday. Yes, on the Other Side. I died. And you know the good thing? I can visit good people and avoid bad ones. And I can find people in Heaven to help me."

I was silent, feeling a bit warmer in general.

"Okay?" he said.

"Yes."

"Sometimes you don't say much," he said.

"Sometimes you ask me to sit here, passive!"

He laughed. "Sorry. Distracted. Ok. Just sit tight."

He got up and coughed and then sat down again.

"What are you doing?" I asked.

"I'm nervous. It's like acting! You can't tell people that by the way. I can't be scared of acting! I'm Patrick Swayze."

I started giggling despite myself. Sometimes he was

insecure about vulnerability and it was charming.

"You know, you could share when you feel vulnerable," I said. "You don't have to be invincible."

"True, Smartypants. I'm just nervous! It's like an audition or something. I have to practice!"

I was really trying not to make it worse by laughing. The absurdity was funny, even though it was becoming increasingly normal.

"What exactly are you acting here?" I asked.

"I don't know. I need a line! Something to say."

"You are always talking!"

"Not true! That actually is not true. I just don't have a sentence right now, you know, for Patrick's first channeled Jodie sentence."

"Oh, I see! For posterity's sake? Ok. Well just say something philosophical and meaningful."

He got up and started to laugh. What a buffoon! I guess we all have our nervous moments, even those who have been in front of the camera for years.

"I'm ready," he said. He sat down.

"I'll go passive," I said.

"Oh, that was loud! Crap! Don't speak when I sit here, it is like you just spoke right into my ear drum!"

"Sorry!" I was instantly passive and silent. And then my body smiled. It was a gleeful little smile, a bit naughty and pleased with itself. It wasn't my smile. I found my mind asking my brain whether it had just sent that command to smile. My brain said no, that wasn't my command. I hadn't smiled. My face had been smiled for me.

"Hello Jodie." There had been a not very pleasant constriction at my throat, and then it had lowered somehow from the inside. Though my face felt more or less the same, I started talking Texan. Thankfully I was on my own. I nearly fainted. "This is profound isn't it? I mean, here I am talking again."

Hearing his voice come out of my mouth, that iconic voice, overwhelmed me more than anything that had happened to date.

"I think this might be the funniest thing that ever happened to me," he said with my voice box. It was one of those moments in life where what you are witnessing is so out of the question to you that all you can do is burst out laughing. I yelped out loud, not in fear, but just in unexpected response to how deeply odd this was. I jumped up and had an involuntary physical reaction, running around the living room like a foolish funky chicken.

"Arghhh!" I shrieked. "That was too, too weird. Don't do it again!" I ran over to the sofa, threw myself on it and hid my head under a cushion.

I could hear him laughing.

"You are really, really Patrick Swayze. Still him!" I shrieked aloud. "I just did your voice!" It wasn't as though I hadn't known it was him. I had stopped questioning it a few weeks ago, but this was some extra level of proof and demonstration that had still managed to shock me. I sat hiding under the cushions in the corner of the room on the nasty little sofa. I was so full of the heebie jeebies that I wasn't coming out.

He said it, he really did. "Nobody puts Baby in the corner."

"Oh, go away!" I shrieked. The heebie jeebies had just upped threefold. "Go away and leave me under these nice cushions!" I was trying to laugh, or scream, or something. But the situation was suddenly so new to my heart that I could do nothing but hide and become the funniest little person he had evidently ever witnessed.

"I'll just sit here and wait then," his voice was warm.

"Excuse me! You just spoke out of me!"

"It was a little strange Jodie yes. But come on now, no need to start acting like a fan!" He was teasing but now I had to hide even more. I felt about the size of a thumb nail.

"I am not a fan!"

"So, grow up and get up and write everything in your little notebook like usual!"

"What's that supposed to mean?" I asked.

"It means live sometimes. Feel. Have reactions. Look like a silly one if you like."

"I don't like!"

"Will you please just let yourself live? You are not even thirty, you little librarian!"

I burst out laughing. I could only be gracious when he had a point, even if my cheeks were a little pink.

"Fine," I said, getting up. "I will go out with my friends and party like it is 1969. You go get in the corner, Baby Swayze."

I gave him that moniker that day, at it stuck.

CHAPTER TWENTY-SIX

I needed a break. I was reading every hour I wasn't working on becoming a better medium. Every hour other than that I was in class, asleep or trying to get myself out for a decent hike. I decided to take an afternoon off reading even if I had to stumble my way through any awkward questions the next day. I wanted to go window shopping, sit in the sun and have a coffee, and spend the rest of the day relaxing my mental energy.

I wasn't used to looking for the spirit worlds outside of the safe haven of the apartment. In the afternoons after class, I tended to tune in on purpose, and almost always Patrick was there with more enthusiasm for teaching and discussion. There was definitely a sense of tuning in, and it was like turning a knob inside my mind that enabled me to see. I didn't know if I was in control of this on and off switch entirely by myself, or if the Other Side could to some extent influence it.

It was a surprise, then when I was downtown in Ithaca, wandering around the main shopping areas, and I heard and saw Patrick beside me.

"Go into that store," he said.

I felt a little bit foolish in the street, talking to someone who I doubted anyone else could see.

"Which?" I said aloud. A woman walking by

looked at me. "Sorry," I said, blushing.

"This is why the spirit world teaches mediums telepathy!" I heard Patrick say. "Let's try to make you not look crazy!"

I wasn't very good at concentrating on hearing in public in the middle of the afternoon.

"I'll talk," he said. "I understand if you don't answer."

I walked into the shop he had pointed out. It sold vintage things, mostly jewellery. I looked around. There were lots of tall glass display cases. Mostly things were not all that expensive. There was a whole array of amber, amethyst, rose quartz and aquamarine.

"Buy a memento," he said. "Just a something. To remember."

I didn't respond instantly, as instructed. It was a sweet idea. I wondered if it was meant as a reminder that the afterlife was real. It occurred to me that Patrick felt quite threatened that I wouldn't speak out about what we'd experienced. I hadn't given a lot of thought to his situation if I simply walked away.

The lady in the shop smiled at me and returned to her paperwork on the counter. I was careful to see she wasn't looking, before I whispered a response.

"What kind of memento?"

"Choose one!" he whispered back and I tried not to laugh.

I looked in the cases. The room was square and

there might have been twelve cases with more in the middle. I worked my way around them and kept coming back to one cabinet. It had several different kinds of crystals in them: agates at the top in the pale colours down to the black tourmalines at the bottom. The middle shelves were jewel tones.

"Buy that ring. I like it," he said. "Treat yourself with a fun ring."

I looked at the case and could sense the one he meant. It was a fairly large purple stone set in gold, or some gold coated metal given the price. It wasn't amethyst. It was too dark. The stone was emerald cut. It was simple but bold.

"What is it?" I whispered.

"I dunno. It looks right."

"Can I help you?" the lady asked.

"May I see this purple ring?" I asked. "Can you tell me what it is?"

"How much?" I heard his whisper.

"And how much is it?"

"It's fifty-five dollars," said the lady as she pulled it from her display. "It's an unusual stone for vintage stores, if not especially valuable. Try it." She held it out. It fit the middle finger of my right hand.

"It is called the mystic's stone, actually," she said. "I have had it a while."

"I've seen it before," he whispered, "in town. I look around while you're in class and things. Tell her you're a medium."

I was really nervous to do that but I did it. "I am a medium," I said. "Perhaps that's why I like it."

She nodded. "Likely it is."

I looked at it on my finger. A random spend of fifty-five dollars plus tax didn't happen very often on my grad school stipend.

"Come on," Patrick whispered. "It's only fifty bucks. Heaven knows you deserve it." He chuckled.

My heart was beating gently, but more noticeably than usual. "Okay," I told the lady. "I'd like to take it."

"Shall I bring you a box?" she said?

"Wear it!" he said. "Or what's the point?"

"I mean, no!" I said. "I won't have a box. I won't waste one. I'll just put it back on."

"Very good." She smiled.

I walked around town the rest of the afternoon, window shopping. I didn't say much to anyone. I could feel Patrick around but I didn't say a lot to him. He seemed to be in peaceful following. Eventually, I found a little coffee shop I liked and sat outside with an iced coffee. There was no-one around and knowing he was there, I asked aloud, "When I am not at class and you are looking around, are you with a lot of other people?"

"No. I only guide you."

"No, I mean, other people who have died. Like Nonny or your own family or maybe friends?"

"Yeah sometimes. Of course. I haven't told you

much about Heaven, huh?"

"No."

"I will. Here's a bit. It's real. We meet our friends. The passed ones of course. And we love new people. People are happy. They have let go of their pains. Their self-doubt. Their lack of self-worth. Their issues. I have met lots of people I love."

"Are they all here walking round Ithaca?"

"No, silly! You would see them. Don't doubt your ability. They cross. I cross back to speak to you and to try to make contact. That's my prerogative. Not everyone wants to or can."

"How come."

"I don't think they believe. Or they can't. Or won't. Nonny says they don't have faith they will be heard, just like living people don't have faith they can hear us."

"When did you know Nonny was my grandma?"

"Before she died. Just before she died."

Nonny had died months after Patrick, aged ninety-four.

I considered this, trying to take it in. I was trying to make order in my mind about something I knew hardly anything at all about. It might be easier not to try, and just to listen.

"How did you meet Nonny?"

"She had crossed by the time I came here, to Ithaca I mean, and she was around you a lot. She looked down on you. I noticed. The dead don't live with the living. I don't like saying the dead. I don't think Lisa would like it somehow. They live in a spiritual plane. Nonny was crossing to see you and so was I."

Somehow, this made reasonable enough sense.

"Thank you, Patrick," I said.

"For?"

"For helping me to understand."

"You're welcome," he said.

"And for choosing this random English woman and persevering with your mission."

"What mission?"

"To prove the afterlife. I mean, isn't that your mission?"

"In a sense. 'Mission' is a strong word. I feel more peace than that. I do now at least. I needed to know that contact could be made. For my own soul. Man, I tried, I really did. With people I knew well. But I travelled to find a link. That link was you. Not too far north, huh?"

"I suppose not."

"And you're welcome. It is important people know and you have been patient. Not patience itself, but patient."

It was hard not to laugh.

"I mean it. Whatever comes next, mediumship or no mediumship, writing or no writing, I am grateful to have life experience that makes me feel alive." I told him the truth. "In my heart and soul, I always felt something like this would happen."

"The heart always knows."

"Perhaps."

"I'm certain. And Jodie. I don't want to push you, but there will be mediumship and there will be books. I am not the only prophet of that. Or mystic. Whatever the term is. Enjoy your ring and accept it. I'm outta here."

I sat in the late sun and drank another iced coffee. Life was something to behold. I offered my gratitude for the gift of life from my heart to whomever might be able to hear it.

The next evening when I walked into the small sitting room with the dining table, I had a surprise. Patrick was there, his denim limbs stretched over the sofa, bare feet. There was a second man sitting on the circular pine table. Patrick was smiling. By this time, I had stopped jumping when I saw his presence, but the other man startled me somewhat.

"The father," the man said. He pointed with his head at Patrick on the sofa. "Of him. We met after his death. You are doing good work."

This second man was also dressed Texas with the shirt and jeans. I saw something in common. They shared those creased eyes and the grin, both charming. Father and son. What an amazing sight.

"You gotta have something to share that people will understand," he told me, drawl. "And you do."

"Hello," I said, softly.

He smiled, and the smile appeared to send light through his heart. "You gotta share what has happened here." He gestured again at Patrick, this time with his thumb. "Or he will give in." I was held still by the sight of them. Patrick had felt always like a presence that was following me. This felt like a visit from somewhere else.

"Patrick is a strong guy, but he is not without his limits."

I continued to look at him.

"My name is Buddy. Buddy Swayze."

"Hi Buddy."

"Jodie the thing is this. People don't die, not really. You gotta tell 'em." He was so clear, I could see every expression line in his face. I could see the colours in his shirt. I could see the grey in his hair.

I nodded at him gently. He seemed like a good man.

"I know," I said quietly.

"Good luck," he said. "You can beat this," he said, pointing at his chest.

"Beat what?" I asked.

"Self-doubt."

I nodded. He had a gentle, fatherly, masculine presence. He said, "He beat it. Buddy over there. My son. But his self-doubt has returned. For you."

I glanced at Patrick, concerned. He was watching, silently and intently.

His father said, "He had a mission and he chose you. I have watched over a little. I've been here a long time. In this world. The other side. Thank you for offering Patrick Swayze a chance to get through." He seemed perfectly comfortable and at ease. "I hope you don't let him down."

He had that same very American voice; very male voice.

"I won't." I said.

"Give yourself ten years. Rome wasn't built in a day."

I smiled at him the best I could. I felt a verbal pact form. One's word is one's bond.

"Excuse me," I said, and left the room gently. I wanted to be in solitude with my soul, and I wanted to give Patrick space with his father.

As I was writing the details of the visit down, I heard Patrick's voice in the hall.

"I trust you." He had said it, finally.

I could have cried.

CHAPTER TWENTY-SEVEN

I was reading when Nonny arrived. It was one of the most tender experiences of my life. I was in the hallway, reading with a highlighter. There was a long-armed lamp reaching over me, and there were many pages left to read. I had highlighted a few lines: two or three sentences from many paragraphs.

She appeared behind me and touched me on both shoulders. My pendulum was in my bag. She came through for the first time without the use of a tool.

I had seen Patrick a lot of times now, but having never known him before he passed, it was less emotional for me to see him. Each time I saw him I was upbeat, pleased, happy that my abilities were developing. He had started to become my friend only after his death. The few people I had told about him, like my best friend, said they believed we had had past lives. Or that we must have met in dreams. I was offered a few ideas to compliment June's, but I was not a researcher and I could not in good faith corroborate or deny any of them. They were nice to think about.

Seeing Nonny was totally different. She had been paramount in my life. I had many, many memories of her from my childhood, from my teenage years and from the years more recently. I had been given a wonderful grandmother. She appeared to come into her own in the role of grandma. Porridge in the mornings, stories, little letters in the post, hugs and kisses. She baked, she laughed, she presented an ease with life that demonstrated as I grew up that all would be alright. She spoke in idioms and what would be called a grandma's wisdom. I remembered the last time I had seen her, and getting up and leaving a class when I got a text at Stanford to say she had died. I had run across a quad to find Edward, who was teaching a class there himself. I had written her eulogy and had spoken at her funeral. Seeing her again in this undoubtable way was enormously emotional for me. Was it the level of emotion involved that had meant I could see Patrick far more easily? Had Patrick been training more in some sense, perhaps as a meditator before his death? Was I able to be more still and peaceful of heart when he was around because I had not personally grieved his death? Perhaps. I wasn't sure.

I followed her into the kitchen.

"I am proud of you," she said. "Do not worry about the small things."

She lifted her hand in the kitchen, palm facing outward. I lifted mine and touched her palm. I could feel her.

She smiled. There was emotion spilling over her lower eyelids. She wiped a tear.

"You'll never fail to surprise me," she said. "Your generation must be strong and challenge everything. But do it in peace. My generation saw so much war."

"I know," I said.

"You know I survived two!" She was born in 1916. World War I and World War II, both of which swept in a very real way through the north of England.

"I know," I said. I wanted to ask her something. "How do you survive a war, Nonny?" I asked.

"Live," she said, with a peaceful smile. "You just live."

She turned, walked away and vanished.

After she left I called Mum. I didn't bother to check the time difference. It wouldn't matter.

"Hello?" she said.

I didn't really know at that point why I had shipped myself to a summer camp to read abstract books few people care about on the other side of the world while my mother had a blood disease in England. I didn't know why I wasn't at home in Yorkshire. I didn't know why I had married someone who, having reflected more and more on it, I thought perhaps had not wanted to be married in the first place. Everything was a little bit off. I was patching, trying to make it all alright. I usually went to my mother for that guidance. Over the years she had been strong with yes and no, and as I grew up she had trained me with the repeated instruction to stay in contact with my heart and to follow it. My flight path was currently way off heart. I knew that more and more because my heart was opening again, and I could hear it once more. My inner and outer worlds were not good representations of each other. I didn't know how to get back on course.

"Hi," I said.

"What's the matter?" she said, concerned from her gift in mother telepathy. It meant I didn't need to try to communicate anything and she still knew.

I started to sniffle and cry down the phone. I had finally broken down.

"Jodie. What is the matter?" Her concern was rising; her volume had risen a bit. "Calm down. Tell me."

"Tell her." I heard Patrick's voice unexpectedly behind me.

"Nonny came to see me."

"What do you mean?" she asked.

"Not with the pendulum. She was just standing there and came to see me. I could see her and talk to her as clear as day. She's really there."

She started to weep too. My mother was also a daughter. She had been very close to Nonny, whose death had been very hard for her. She missed her every day. "Well, what did she say?"

"Nothing to upset me. But it's just such a lot. I don't know why I am crying really." I wiped my tears and started to get it together.

"I think you have been given a special gift. I don't know why. But you have." Her voice was soft and teary.

"I know," I said. "Another gift to understand. That God is busy with me." I had tried to bring a chuckle.

"Do you believe in God?" Religion was something we never really spoke about. Or faith, regardless of a creed.

"I don't know. Do you?"

"Yes. I think so. As I get older. I do. I didn't when I was with your father. But my time on my own has given me time to find my own way."

I needed to be with that comment for a little while. "What are you doing?" I asked.

"Watching a film. Something about Reno. It has Patrick Swayze in it. He just seems to be on whenever I turn on the TV."

"Coincidence." I said.

"I suppose," she replied. "When are you going home?" she asked.

"At the end of the week. I'm going straight. No trips."

"Right," she said. "When does term start this year?"

"About the 20th September." I had a deep need to be with my mother. I tried not to cry again. "Can you perhaps come out in the next month to California?"

"I'll try. I was going to go to Austria."

"Can you and Christine come here instead? I'll take you both on a tour of California. If she is well enough."

"Well that would be nice. Ok. I will talk to her. She should be okay to travel. Will you have time with your work?"

"Yes, I'll make it up."

"Ok!" she seemed excited. "Is Nonny there now?"

"Do you believe me that I'm a medium?" I answered, feeling like a little girl.

"Yes!" she said. "What a silly thing to make up. Don't be silly. I knew you were different."

"Thanks. I don't think she is here, no. She's more likely to be with you."

"Probably. Maybe she comes to see each of us each week."

"I don't know how she does all that transatlantic travel!" I said. I hadn't yet tried to fathom how she might be overseeing Austria one day and at New York State the next. I just knew the information she was giving about both locations was dead on. Astral travel and the travel of the spirit planes were topics I knew nothing about. I could feel the pressure of ignorance.

"I miss her. I wish I could hear," Mum said.

"I'll try to teach you. I don't know how. But I can try."

"Don't worry. You can tell me what she says. Don't pressure yourself too much. You always do that."

"Ok." We both knew I would pressure myself. It had been a theme over twenty-nine years.

"Is Edward okay?"

"Think so," I said.

"I see." She was quiet for a second. "If it's not to be, it's not to be."

"I love him."

"Yes, I know. And he you. But something isn't right. I will see more if I come to visit, hey? Hard to be so far from my little girl."

"Ok, come."

"Jodie, you must do something with it. The mediumship. People don't all get gifts like you have just been given. And I believe you about Patrick, but people will want to know. You must be honest and be brave."

"I know."

"You know I have brought you up to be those things," she said.

Soon after, we hung up, hoping to see one another soon.

Honest and brave. Did I need to hear it from many more directions?

With only a few days to go in Ithaca, I kept to myself and worked hard on taking as many notes as I could for my Stanford work. When I felt I had fulfilled that duty, I filled as many notebooks as I could with every memory, sensation and experience I had had over the last six weeks. Patrick had told me that he wanted me to write about this time in my life. He wanted it out there. He wanted people to be asked to think about these things. He had some passion about it. Observing I was calmer than him about it, I felt that he really just wanted to encourage research and, ultimately, for people to wake up to Spirit. He used that phrase.

I was far from committed to a book. But I took the notes. I was sitting one afternoon in the study in the hallway in the apartment. I was writing everything down. Faintly at first, and then with more clarity, a song was sung in my mind. I grasped at it, and it rose in my consciousness like a volume dial slowly being turned to full. It came in at a half-line. "... *the place I'm supposed to be./ On and on and on I've searched/ What I'm looking for is not here on earth./ I can't stand...*" I recognized it. Macy Gray, from an album I played and sung in the car in California, still stuck on 90s music. I sang along in my mind softly to the words I knew, guessing at the parts I didn't. *"Down here in reality, everybody knows there aint no such thing./ And it's clear..."* I loved that album. Patrick must have heard me play it recently.

The message was from him. I got up and looked up the lyrics to Macy Gray's *The Letter*. The song seemed so pertinent. Copyright means I can't quote a whole song, but I would here if I could. I hope those who can find a message in it of hope and positivity do read all the lyrics online. I knew Patrick wanted to talk to his fans. To me, that he had chosen this song was so perfect.

All I ever wanted was some love and peace and harmony,
I could dance in the raw in the sun underneath the stars.
When I walk over to my money tree, aint nobody there
Trying to take from me
When they ask 'Are you truly free?' I'd say 'Yes, truly'."

I read poetry of it several times. I played the song. I felt the emotion of every line.

So long everybody.

I knew it was over. Holding it together was over. The cruelty of this, the bitter cruelty of death. The love that still lived, and the peace. The separations and the challenges. The efforts for communication. The oneness with the world. Bittersweet in the very essence of the world.

I cried for him, really cried for him, for the first time. For what he must have been through in his cancer, for his loss of life, and for the family that lost him. Perhaps, I thought later, even for what he and I were going through, and what might come when I announced my knowledge of the afterlife. *Everybody knows there aint no such thing.*

Still upset, I looked at quotes from Patrick himself online. There was a page of things he had said over the years. One stood out to me.

I keep my heart and my soul open to miracles.

CHAPTER TWENTY-EIGHT

It was the night that the hundred and fifty or so participants of the summer program would go to a dinner up at Cornell to receive certificates for attending. Somehow, I had completed the course, noted chapters, and had even had half an hour with one of the acclaimed visiting professors. She had smiled, advised, and liked my thesis ideas enough to instill some confidence. She had a deep twinkle in her eye that made me think for a second that if I just sat and told her this whole series of recent events, she might actually be someone who would listen. But I didn't say a word on the subject. Before she dismissed me for the next student in the line outside her door, she said something that stuck in my mind. She said the job of the English professor was to prove that the world has meaning, and to demonstrate it. The job was to find that meaning in a professional way.

I got ready for the dinner, put a nice dress on, did my hair and looked at myself in the mirror. I didn't go. My heart wouldn't let me. I was still trying to work out quite where I stood now, as though my feet were hovering over a big chess board and I was not sure which piece I was, how it moved, or where it fit with the others. Was I a knight or a castle? I had swotted for maybe fifty exams to find myself sitting in Ithaca. I thought I had read maybe two thousand books. I had taught other people's words, underlined other people's words, judged them and admired them and given my entire vocational life to them. I had lived in other people's characters. I had quoted other people's words and considered their perspectives. I had been setting myself up for an entire career of them. Suddenly I knew with finality that that was no longer going to happen for me in this life. I wanted my own words.

I announced it to the air. Edward called me, asking me if about my flight details the next day. I told him that Ph.D. or no Ph.D., there would be no academic job, no wife professor. It was my safety net, I told him, and I was not going through life in a safety net any more.

It was not a conversation that left me with a lot of hope in our marriage. I had hope in him. I had hope in myself again. I just felt sick that my hope in the us was shrinking.

I had worked less hard than my friends during this class, and I didn't feel it was appropriate for me to show up to receive a certificate. I went and ate dinner downtown instead.

There was a party at one of the professor's houses after the formal ceremony. I arrived at that and made my polite excuses. My friends showed concern that I hadn't been there, as did our summer professor, but she let it go. I thanked her for the course and the rich environment of her classroom. She had lots of other students to say goodbye to, and she left me alone other than when she pulled me into the group photo.

"You may have missed the celebration," she said, "but you were a part of our class. No summer would be the same without any of the students we chose."

We were at peace. "Thank you. As far as I can see, this is the celebration!" There was a whole table of nice wine, and a hoard of students who didn't see that very often. The cups were glass, not paper. The desserts to go with the after-dinner drinks were not store bought. Someone had taken some time to create something special. "Is this your home?" I asked.

"Yes." She took my shoulder. "Please, Jodie, listen. Good luck in the world." She gave me a light, professorial hug, and turned to make her way to the table of wine.

I had an unexpected tear. I didn't know if I had just been given my exit card from academia, but it felt like it. It was a key, not a dismissal slip. It felt like someone with authority in my life was trying to stand as the jailor who broke in and opened the gates to the prison. She hadn't forced me out, but she had slipped a key into my hand and had turned and walked away. She had reminded me of free will, however deep into a situation we might be. It had been a decade of my life. Every decision—financial, familial, intellectual, emotional. The Professor in English. I had wanted it since I had first met a professor at Cambridge and had felt a deep sense of home.

I made light small talk with some of the girls on the course, barely hearing their questions. I asked Paul and Mike if we could go, finished my drink, and was happy to find they were glad to join me at one of the bars downtown for a drink.

We walked across town, and mostly I listened to the stories of the certificate ceremony and Paul and Mike's comments on the likely professional future of some of our class. It was always who was mostly like to lecture at Harvard, or the other Ivy League universities. That was the holy grail. I listened to them talk about the various projects of everyone, and I mostly stayed quiet. Paul finally asked why I had missed the ceremony.

"I just felt terrible," I said. "I couldn't be there."

"You look okay. Better, I think," said Mike.

"Thanks. I am okay." I wanted to change the subject while we walked, and asking to see their certificates was enough. They both had a deep sense of pride for having completed this prestigious course. They were trying to cover it, educated in humility as they both were, but it shone from their eyes as though they were two excited little boys. They had worked hard this summer, and had read thousands and thousands of pages. I offered them a drink on me.

"Will Edward mind if you take two handsome men for a drink?" said Mike.

"I doubt it," I said.

"Is everything ok?" asked Paul.

"We'll see. He's a good guy."

"That doesn't mean. . ." Paul had begun but was interrupted by Mike.

"Let it be. It's celebration night!" Mike was smiling in sunbeams. He had found his purpose.

We sat with drinks in the same place I had been sick. Having listened to their talk for half an hour, I could remember so clearly why I had wanted the life they had both chosen. They spoke about university professor life with the same ideals I once had, and I found it balmy to hear it, whatever my own situation. The working life is such glue. I found myself trying it on again, their idea of the future. Walking away, to them, might be like training for ten years to be a surgeon and then never performing a surgery.

The image of the professorial life felt like home again as I listened. I could see it. I could see myself doing well there. Then the more we talked, and the more I heard their enthusiasm and daydreams, that home became the exterior of the home, then the facade of a house, a stuck-on stucco exterior. Then it fell away to leave unprotected rooms facing the elements. I didn't belong in an academic setting. It had been the five-year plan, and the thirty-year plan. Now I knew I didn't have one. I didn't want to face the elements for my whole life, however many years I had already put into the training.

But I liked these people. I really did, the two of them. I told them I didn't think university life was for me any longer. Paul was shocked. Mike nodded and said he had noticed all class that I had been trying to pull away. After a glass of wine, he told me that he'd resented it at first. I'd been given a world class education through two of the world's top places of education. And he had resented that I wouldn't put that back into the university system. Paul told him to back down. He had a soft, protective streak in his heart under all those hours in the gym. I wanted to hug him and make his perfect wife and home and family appear with a click of the finger. He deserved it. Mike interjected. He said that he had already had a change of heart. He had become my friend over the pineapple wine on the wine tour. He understood that it's not right to keep someone where they don't belong.

He asked me what was next then, would I finish my PhD? I said yes, I thought that I would. I still cared about scholarship. I didn't know for certain what I'd work on yet. It had to be something that I could feel would link the ivory tower to normal everyday people. To people who still read books for leisure. To people who validate the whole book industry by buying books.

He didn't care about my answer really. He was more interested in where my true passion was.

"Not sure," I said. "I think I might be a medium."

"What?!" Paul almost spat his wine out in surprise.

"I'm not all that surprised," said Mike. "There is

something about you. Something, I don't know. Otherworldly. I'm not flirting now. But 'otherworldly' is my term."

I felt accepted, and just that micro-dose of it was enough to make me smile from the heart.

"I didn't know 'otherworldly' was a flirting word," I said.

Paul laughed. "Come on! We know he loves that Star Wars girl."

"Well I love that you are a dork, Mike." Just his acceptance had given me hope. We ordered more wine.

"I love that you are a dork, man," Paul said. "I'll have a martini, no wine."

"You do?" Mike said, "Thanks. You think it disguises my little tummy?" They laughed. I wished I could keep them both. We'd be scattered across the country tomorrow.

Mike was clearly going to run a department some day in a good university, but he would still get you with his light saber.

"Thank you for being my friend all summer," I said to Paul. "You're a rock." He had had the most lunches and dinners with me of anyone. He had held my hair back when I was sick.

"Welcome."

He looked at me. "You're likely one of the smartest guys in the class. . ." I said.

"Agreed," said Mike.

"But don't be a professor. You're too, um, well-adjusted."

We all burst out laughing. How could we have so much love for a profession and at the same time want to run away?

"We will see. I have a plan B."

"I hope it's beautiful babies," said Mike.

"It's the police force," said Paul.

Mike mused silently.

"Jodie," Paul said. "Are you really a medium? Like, dead people?"

I looked at him and saw myself in his eyes, but myself all those weeks ago, and all those years ago, when I hadn't been transformed by Patrick Swayze. When I hadn't been transformed from over-analytical to someone more balanced, more of the heart. More willing to accept life beyond the intellect. I had affection for that version of me I saw in his questioning eyes, which longed to understand, and yet I knew she was no longer with me.

"Yes. Like dead people."

"Seriously? Man. I don't think I believe in that stuff. I mean, sure. I haven't really thought about it," Paul answered.

"If she can do it, it's real." said Mike.

"Thank you. You're sweet," I said.

We poured wine and sipped and compared tasting notes vis-a-vis the wines on our tour. We had no idea what we were doing. It was all phony theatre, but light-hearted. Then, Mike suddenly said.

"You can see Patrick Swayze, can't you?"

I just looked at him.

"Yeah," he said. I thought so. "I had a dream after the Point Break movie. Never mind."

"Tell me."

"Nah. It just came back to me. He'll be around." The emotions in his eyes was intense. "Good luck my friend."

"Wow," said Paul. He had sunk his martini in one. It took something to get him from his head to his heart and soul, but they were all three good. "I'll have a final martini."

We pledged a solidarity that night, the three of us. I felt each of us would go in different directions, into physical worlds that might not naturally cross, and they might not socially cross. It made me sad. But I felt somehow, in some version of this mysterious universe, we would all continue to buoy each other from afar when it came to the heart and spirit.

CHAPTER TWENTY-NINE

I woke having slept badly. I had slept later than I had planned by an hour. My plane was at three, from Ithaca Tompkins to Detroit to San Francisco. I hadn't packed. I hadn't cleaned the apartment. I still had food in the fridge and flowers on the table. My books were still on the desk. I hadn't yet made any gesture to signal that I was leaving. I hadn't even checked in. All I had was a printed sheet with my flight details on. Waking slowly, I felt groggy, like I had been somewhere else far away while I was sleeping. It seemed to take forever to open my eyes. My watch said it was eleven. Eleven! My body wanted to move fast, but my soul felt slow. I was trying to render something, to bring something into my brain from my astral state, but it left me. You can condition the mind to remember sleep time activity with lucidity, but I hadn't begun that training.

Before I got out of bed I called and ordered a taxi for half past one. I'd just make the flight. I had two and a half hours to pack, clean and say goodbye.

Reluctantly, I got up for the last time in the apartment that overlooked the carpark. I got out of the bed and stripped it. My mind wanted stillness, so I could make some mental decisions over the next hour or two, and find words to say. But my emotional were in a panic because of the clock of the wall, and as a result I felt like I was almost watching my body as it functioned on the adrenaline of poor timing. I grabbed a robe, ran out of the door to the shared laundry on the landing and put the sheets in to wash with a few quarters. I dug for those quarters in my purse as other coins fell all over the floor. I would leave the engineering student the sheets and the vase and a few other things, hoping he wouldn't mind a few gifts. At least they would be clean. I put the shower on to warm and pulled my suitcase out from under the bed. I started throwing things into it, unfolded. Who cared? I'd wash everything at home, or get rid of some of the old stuff. In the past couple of days, I'd noticed I had lost about six of the ten pounds that had crept on during the past year at Stanford, when my life and heart had become sedentary. There were the books everywhere in the apartment. I couldn't work out in my rush how I would get all the new books from Cornell home with me via two airports. I still didn't go online to check in.

I jumped in the shower, washed my hair, scrubbed the bath while I was still in it, and ran around in a towel wiping surfaces. I threw some things away from the big old refrigerator and left a note saying to please keep all the in-date food and the wine that wasn't opened. It felt like giving my home away.

I dragged a black bag of rubbish out into the entry way, still in my towel. I threw books into my carry-on bag, which had no wheels. It looked heavy and too full. I threw them all over the floor and started again. I didn't need them but what could I do with them? They'd break my back running across Detroit airport, I knew it. But I couldn't leave them unwanted. For me, a book has always had a soul.

Finally, at half past twelve, with the kitchen still not cleaned and my mental eye on the deposit cheque, I picked up the moonstone at the kitchen. I still had that original piece of paper, folded into four, with the letters in bold black ink. It was dirty after six weeks, but still somehow sacred.

The pendulum moved again. I wasn't expecting it. N-O-N-N-Y.

"Nonny?" It swung backwards and forwards. I looked around for her and saw her but she was outlined in silver with sparkles. She didn't look like she had done. There was just a silver, glittery outline that I knew to be her, and she appeared a little bit bigger. They say this is the spirit body.

Y-O-U-A-R-E-P-R-E-C-I-O-U-S.

The second hand on the clock in the living room told me not to cry. But still.

"Thank you."

G-O-O-D. V-E-R-Y-G-O-O-D.

Her voice was breaking through to me. I was so used to talking to her via the pendulum that I had already formed a meaningful tradition around it. I thought she said good work this summer and to keep going. There were too many emotions in me for me to have a sound response to that. Before she died, she had celebrated me getting a scholarship to Stanford, and had cried every time I got on the plane back to California, always asking me if she would ever see me again. I had never let her see me cry, but had cried as soon I was out of the eye view of her and my mother. I had always told myself that I was crossing the world away from them to give myself a chance to give something to the world. In England, we just didn't have the money supporting the arts disciplines in universities. I wasn't yet sure if we had the culture to support mediumship in the north of England either, but I felt some peace knowing that in California there would people I could share my experiences with via research groups and metaphysical conferences.

I put the pendulum down and scrubbed the kitchen sink and tops. I dried my hair and donated the hair dryer to the bathroom cupboard. I hoped the lease guy wouldn't judge me for leaving him these touches of femininity.

The vacuum cleaner was terrible but I got around the apartment with it. The taps weren't chalky any more. The wardrobe now had hangers. The curtains hung a little straighter. The sofa had been vacuumed. The spiders had had time to make new homes. The ancient webs had finally been dusted away.

There was still bolognese on the floor. Tomato.

I had to pack the pendulum and it seemed silly and sentimental to keep the piece of paper. I went to throw it away and then stopped and opened it again. It was such a simple technology. It felt to me that sometimes there are people out there in the world, and if not still of this living world then of the wider universe, that might see us in some moments more clearly than anyone else every has. More than family, more than friends. I felt deeply that I knew they were out there. We just didn't have the all technologies of communication. Perhaps Facebook offered the link to some people—it was a mechanism to bring you people you might need but wouldn't otherwise find. It had been that sometimes to me. The mind, I knew, was another link. Any seasoned medium could show that. I deeply wanted to support new technologies of communication that could bring more guidance, trust and closeness back into our world. Holding that moonstone, I saw the link between the aspects of my life and the activities that seemed like disparate callings of my heart. The book, the pendulum, the mind. I had started to study and champion them all because they all had the power to break down walls in pursuit of a higher good. Walls that come from lack of knowledge, or fear, or missing concepts. I believed more and more in crumbling them. They are all walls that separate the heart from other hearts, and some great universal heart that I could feel must be out there.

In that moment, my tool of communication was a pendulum, and I had a voice to use. Nonny used to say to me, when she had been alive, "Do you have a throat? Use it. Speak."

The pendulum started to swing in circles, faster and faster, and then so fast that it flung from my hand and hit the wall.

I jumped, scared, and ran to retrieved it. It was chipped slightly but it had survived.

I heard the voice. Soft. I didn't know the voice. "You are better than this tool, the moonstone. The energy of some in spirit is so strong that it will break. Your arm will ache. Think of love when you channel and all will be good. You have the power to channel for anyone you choose. We are proud of you in heaven." Whose was this beautiful voice? "I love you. I love all. You are becoming a strong and true spirit. Be cautious and noble sometimes. Be true and honest with others. Be love and yet look to your own self sometimes. But always, always be the truth. The truth is your key to eternity. Use it." The voice came softly over and around me. It was saintly and unexpected. It went on, "Your grandmother would like you to go forward. Patrick would like you to research. I would like you to follow your path, which will call you to it as mine did and as theirs did and does. Do good. Serve God. Be gone from here."

His energy and presence completely left the room.

A call to serve the divine. I had been asked to face my vacillating agnosticism and atheism. I had always been polite to any believer, and unsure of my own beliefs. I knew now for sure that there is consciousness beyond the physical plane, and that there is a real life after death. But serve God? What did that even mean? Who was God? What was God? Was there a servant in me? I didn't know. I just didn't. I would have to go back to California, to the secular, academic, empiricist life that I had been living outwardly, stand still for a while, and then hope this message were true and I would find my rightful path. I can tell you that I was terrified. But I had two options before me, and I had avoided both for a lot of years: terror and faith. I hoped I could align myself to the latter.

There were twelve minutes to go before the taxi was due. Finally, I sat on the little box sofa and waited. And I waited. There were six minutes to go before I saw Patrick move across the room. He appeared in the middle of the dining table and walked out through the corridor, unaware it seemed of the laws of the physical dimension. As though he had been in another plane that people write of, some plane I had been in in my sleep. Perhaps they call it heaven. He was all outlined in silver like Nonny, not in colour. He was himself, still the same unmistakable face, but now as I saw him he was pictured in white and clear silhouettes with a solid thin silver edge. He was definitely immune to the physical dimensions of the table from this plane he was visiting from, but he acknowledged the entry space into the hallway that had been my study. He seemed to check to see if the books had gone.

I heard one word in his voice.

"Pendulum!" It was plaintive.

The Indian special stone. My precious link to the impossible. To hope. Had I arrived in Ithaca as a being who found it difficult to hope? Had faith been too hard? Yes, I think both thoughts were somewhat true. Yet this stone, found in the seam when I was meant to be reading, had brought me a whole new world. It had showed me the seams that linked a great patchwork quilt. A sacred world beyond the senses. It had linked to another sense and had left me this sense as a new gift. I was sad it had been chipped.

I felt certain that I live in a world in which there where thousands of us—millions—who could each and every one find their own simple and easy tool to cross a miraculous bridge. It didn't need to be to the afterlife. That was the particular miracle that had come to me, and I could now stand for it for myself and bring it to others. Someone else's bridge could be a bridge to just about anything to make a more marvelous world. I had worked in universities and publishers my entire life up to that point—both places determined to deliver new knowledge and new meaningful stories to the world. Looking at Patrick I felt that I had finally been given that new knowledge and a new story—I had just needed to open my vision a little bit on my everyday path through life. I marveled at the amazing, intelligent, living tapestry we call life. I had been one thread in Patrick's Bayeaux. He had been in mine. In fact, he had sown his own little corner. He didn't really need to say anything. I could feel what his heart was asking, and I could finally see what it has been asking when he had first appeared some weeks ago. I could see why he has been frustrating. He had come from a heaven to verify it to the living and to stand for a place of love that he had witnessed. It filled his perspective. I felt sorry that in my ignorance and fear and frustration I had brought him to some frustration too. I could see that he had helped me make huge breakthroughs in recognizing him as a loving presence, a soul built for love. Like all souls. I knew he had been to such a place, where all was love. And I knew that he was asking me to share it in a cynical world, knowing that every soul in it was, in fact, made of love. He wanted me to ask people to build those bridges to make the living world its own kind of heaven.

I wrote my impressions down. He glowed with a bright gold color and disappeared from my sight. I didn't know where to. I was still for thirty seconds or so, so I moved, getting ready to leave.

"Jodie?"

I looked up from putting my boots on.

"Jodie, it's Nonny, can you hear me?"

The voice seemed distant from me. But I heard it clearly. There appeared to be sensors to her voice in my heart. I looked around the room and couldn't see her.

"Go on! Be at peace! Make marvels! The world needs the believers. Then the universe, well, don't be scared when you die. There is so much more, so, so much more to come."

I could have offered myself to the angels of death right then. For the first time, I saw perhaps there might be angels at death. I saw death was nothing to fear and that it is senseless to live a life just to avoid death. Just as clearly, I saw my life force wanting me to be here, alive, contributing, but maintaining my link to Heaven. My soul still had many things to do here alive. It was wonderful to feel that positive message come from within my being.

"I love you!" Nonny said.

I could have given a million dollars to hear that beautiful phrase from my grandmother's voice. I didn't have that money, but I had been given my own special gift. And it had come for free.

I put my hands together and looked to the heavens.

"Thank you!" I couldn't help but bow. What force was out there? I didn't know. But I was moved to bow to it.

You might have guessed I was scared to address Patrick. I didn't fear his recrimination that I was going back to my marriage, to my life of finishing my PhD, and of not yet quite believing in the higher powers, though I was getting closer. I feared what I would feel when I looked at him and told him I was about to live those things. A likely mediocrity. I felt that he would have some understanding or at least acknowledgment, given his humanity. But I feared my own heart would crumble in the face of my own weaknesses, and that my heart might hope for a better or different human to walk around in. I feared he would see that. I didn't know totally clearly yet precisely why he had appeared to me of all people, but I knew some of the patterns of life. We meet people sometimes whose job it is, whether they know it or not, to call out our hearts. They are a part of life and they offer the door to the deeper gifts. Patrick had been such a spirit to me. I was nervous now to let him down.

I couldn't see him as I was gathering my bag to go. But I felt a presence, the same one I had felt the first day I had moved into this apartment for the summer. I now knew its essence, and I knew it was Patrick's essence.

I said something aloud that surprised me. I felt teary, as though rivers could run from my heart. "I am grateful to your wife. She is a part of who you are. Make sure she knows. Make sure she knows what is possible." I didn't know where I got this information or impression from other than from writing down many positive things. It seemed to open me to a sort of universality, in which I could see the link between the two of them.

"Might *you*?" I heard his voice. "Tell her?"

"I don't know. Yes. No." We have lives, and people ask us for great things, and the chaos, or the minutia, or the routine, or the rigour of life get in the way.

Or the abject fear and worry.

"Sit down," he said. *Sit daahhn.* So drawl.

I did it.

What was I going to do about my entire life? He seemed to feel the question on my heart.

"Live. Do the right thing. Be happy."

His message was so universally simple and moving that it brought more tears to my eyes.

Then I said, "Horse. Shit." I giggled. I was remembering seeing him spell that to me on the pendulum. "Horse! Shit!" I giggled again. My mind was full of the dung as I tried to use it to sort out my heart.

"Pardon?" I saw him then, in colour. Almost as a living person, opaque and real. The face, the hair, the too big shirt. The half-smile. No silvers or whites. He had crossed back, I suppose, for a second more.

"Do the right thing that suits your soul, and remember all good memories when you need them!" I chuckled too. It was music to hear.

There was nothing left in the apartment other than he and I looking at each other and my bags by the door. There was a tear from his eye. Another. Looking at him was like looking at the face of my best friend in the universe, but a friend I would never be able to claim as my own. He belonged to too many people for someone small like me. That's what I thought. Not just his wife and family. But to his fans. To his millions of fans. And, of course, to Heaven. To the grandeur of Heaven in its sunset colours.

My heart was so pulled that I could feel it reaching out of my body. The heart is beyond the body. It can travel beyond. I felt it in a literal way. *Stay*, it said to me. *Make something possible.*

I couldn't meet it. I couldn't quite meet the power of my heart. I still hope to, these years later.

I spent several still seconds just looking at those eyes. The eyes are the contact point, they really are. More than the body.

"I wish I'd met ya," he mumbled. "You would have been my friend."

"Aren't I?"

It started to crumble, that heart in my chest. It felt like a massive open hole. I could literally feel movement in it. I hadn't got any words to go with it. I could feel the pressure of invisible souls screeching at me. *Do something!* What was I going to do? Walk through the veil with him and help bring love to people? Make them see there is so much more than the everyday? How?

I had to face my life. I was three years and a summer into a six-year degree. I lived among people for whom my experiences would be untenable. I knew it and I knew that I would not be wrong about their likely cynicism. I didn't know what would come next. I didn't want my memories here with Patrick to be tainted by what might come next, and I didn't want him to have to visit communities without belief.

For the memories, I picked up the moonstone and I let it wave a bit. He had hated communicating through it. It was lesser than his spirit.

I tried a smile. It didn't work without tears.

"What is going to happen?" I asked him.

"Pick it up again."

He reached and touched the pendulum. The stone moved slightly. Another miracle that did nothing to stop my tears. He gestured at my bag, unable to speak himself. I brought him the letters on the old piece of paper. They were not thrown away, instead destined for my old wooden memory box. I put the paper on the old round pine table.

I-D-O-N-T-K-N-O-W.

He didn't make eye contact with me. He gestured back to the pendulum and nodded at me to read from it and to write the letters down.

I-L-L-S-E-E-Y-A.

He put a hand on my shoulder for a moment then turned and walked toward his window. This time he walked straight through it and was gone.

The taxi pulled up outside. The driver silently put my bags in the car. He could see my tears. I didn't look back. I cried all the way to the airport. When I got out of the car, I was creased in the middle, crying silently from everywhere. A presence appeared with me, tall and powerful. It seemed to encase me, holding me together. It was not Nonny, and it was not Patrick. It was something otherworldly, angelic. It brought me to a sort of anesthetized calm so I could manoeuvre through check in. In the bathroom at the airport, I went to wash my hands and looked in the mirror. For a flash, I saw the face of the saintly man in the mirror. Onlooking, he gave a benevolent half smile, a nod of the head, and he turned and walked away into the depth of the mirror. Then, looking back at me were the strongest pair of blue eyes I had ever seen, just next to me. They were from somewhere else, some other plane. I needed strength and found some by looking into them.

There was a gentle voice. "I am Michael. You must go on."

EPILOGUE

Over the next years, many of the things I had been warned of in Ithaca came true. My husband and I separated, and I lost my mother to leukemia a few months before my scheduled Ph.D. graduation. I delayed graduation a year so I could go back to England and spend her last month with her. By that point, I had had to prove the gifts of mediumship to myself, and had started offering readings around my Stanford work. I offered readings on both sides of the Atlantic and by the time my mother died I had given a thousand of them. I was fully booked everywhere I went: the information for people poured through me and increasingly people started to note and speak of the presence of angels. On the day of my mother's death, I was warned her death was coming by the spirit of my great grandmother. I was with my mother for her final hours and watched her move from this physical plane into the heavens. It was the greatest loss of my life, and one of the hardest things to experience, and yet my clairvoyance enabled me to witness her subtle bodies leaving the physical body seconds before the heart monitor flat-lined. I truly watched her leave the room with Nonny. My grief that followed my mother's death was intense and lingering—a whole new beast to get to know and struggle with. But the gift I was opened to in Ithaca and my decision to follow it in good faith made it so much easier that it could have been. I am still able to communicate with her and so do almost daily.

I finished my PhD at Stanford that year later than expected, and was proud of my work. It was rewritten as my first book, *The Bestseller Code*, along with one of my Stanford professors. My spiritual work for other people continued. I stopped for some periods to research metaphysical experiences and theory so that I could teach and understand some of what I was experiencing. In early 2017, I was awarded a BSc in Metaphysical Science, and the PhD is pending. I am so grateful that there are now formal opportunities to study metaphysics and that the wider culture is starting to open to the research and discussion. My work with people internationally as a channel and link to the heavens led to the moniker Channel of Heaven, and I still work in that way as much as I can. It has been enormous personal growth, in and out, and as a result I feel more able to help other people awaken to their spirits.

Patrick continued and continues to visit. Over the years perhaps ten mediums have witnessed him around me. He is committed to research and practice of meditation, new healing methods and metaphysical research, and often brings me new information. He is a much-loved soul. He speaks fondly of his family and his fans, and with much gratitude for the life he made from the gifts he was given.

Patrick pushed me to write this book for seven years. Given my mother's death, the deaths of three other people I was very close to, a divorce, and the demands of the academic side of my life, there were a few false starts. In the end, I wrote it back in the town I was born in England, surrounded by notebooks. Each and every notebook I opened reminded me of the possibility of miracles, even if they work out differently than we might have planned ourselves.

Patrick has read every word of *I Say Tomato*. Or tom-A-toe, as he would say.

Thank you for reading. May your own journey be blessed.

NB: Names of friends have been changed throughout this book to protect their privacy.

SONG LIST

I write with music. Many of my books come with playlists that readers might chose to play through Apple Music or equivalent with their own subscriptions. I hope they add something to your reading. My playlist for *I Say Tomato* is shared on Apple Music. It is called I Say Tomato Book Patrick Swayze. For this book, it felt right to let you know which song goes with each section of the book.

ARRIVAL IN ITHACA
1) Stranger in Moscow – Michael Jackson
NONNY COMES THROUGH
2) Make You Feel My Love – Adele
PATRICK MAKES CONTACT
3) If You're Out There – The Dartmouth Cords
WAS THIS REALLY HIM?
4) Let's Call the Whole Thing Off – Fitzgerald & Armstrong
WAKING UP
5) Thinkin Bout You – Frank Ocean
OPENING THE SOUL
6) Unwritten – Natasha Beddingfield
THE FIRST READING
7) I'm Coming Out – Diana Ross
LEARNING CONTACT
8) Tears in Heaven – Eric Clapton

CHANGE BECKONS
9) Sparks – Coldplay
PATRICK ON HIS FANS
10) The Letter – Macy Gray
THE HUG & THE TEARS
11) Forever Young – Rod Stewart
TIME FOR RETURN
12) I've Had the Time of my Life – Bill Medley & Jennifer Warnes

ACKNOWLEDGMENTS

Everyone mentioned in this book has my heartfelt gratitude for living these experiences with me, and for listening as I went through the experience of opening to my spirit. I am grateful for the compassion and support I received in the unique ways of each and every one of you. You are always in my heart.

After Ithaca, I started offering spiritual readings for people. I stood up and shared my experiences in living rooms in California and in England. Soon, I had appointment diaries that were full for months, and that curiosity and support from strangers and people I barely knew gave me the reason and encouragement to keep going, to keep practicing, and to develop my research. It is not always easy to be the "different one". I had shut down my ability as a child, and once or twice since Ithaca I almost shut it down again. But there were enough thoughtful and caring people out there who believed in the afterlife, in me, and in Patrick Swayze, that I kept going. I am grateful to every person who has come to me for a reading, who has bared their soul and shared their fears, and has let me witness their tears of joy, sorrow, and of the confusing moments that hit us all on the journey of being a human being… Or a spiritual being on a human journey. Thank you to all those who support the sincere research and demonstration of metaphysical abilities. Humanity has so much to gain from investment in this research, and from all efforts to link disciplines in research—philosophy, religion, science, literature, politics, and metaphysical science.

For one reason or another, all of which have seemed in some sort of divine order, it took me seven years to turn this book from journals into a book to share with people. During those years I lost some people who were very dear to me. During my first couple of years at Stanford, I lost my paternal and maternal grandmothers. After Ithaca, I lost Gisela Umpleby, my third grandmother figure, to cancer of the brain. I lost David Taylor, who was a second father figure to me. He had suffered from, among other things, prostate cancer. I lost a childhood friend who was my age, Edward Watson, to a rare form of lung cancer. I had not seen him latterly, but as children and early teens we had been close. He had a starred first-class degree from Cambridge and his death was a terrible shock to so many of us. I worked for a while at Apple, who lost Steve Jobs to pancreatic cancer. Patrick Swayze had also died of pancreatic cancer.

The loss of my mother Linda to cancer of the blood was somehow, despite all you have read, one of the most shocking things I have ever experienced. Seeing Nonny and Patrick visiting from Heaven felt shocking but natural to me. Watching people die from this terrible condition was shocking and deeply unnatural to me. I can verify an afterlife, but that does not mean I don't believe in all research that might prevent premature deaths. As a conduit, I have spent time as a healer and a medium listening to everything the higher planes could tell me, in the time I had, about possible cures for aspects of cancer. Guided, I have been involved in three profound healings, but I was unable to save my mother. I am grateful to everyone who supports alternative and metaphysical research, because people will change lives with that research. It needs some more formalized support.

I am of course also grateful to the wonderful people who are fighting cancer in medical wards. Ten percent of all proceeds of this book will go to The Pancreatic Swayze Pancreatic Cancer Research Fund and Stanford University. A further ten percent will go to the Annette Fox Leukaemia Research Fund at Ward 7 at the Bradford Royal Infirmary. That was the ward that lovingly took care of my mother after her funding for private care ran out.

We are all trying to make the world a better place. Thank you.

My dear, sweet Nonny. What can be said? I love you more than all the tea in China and all the coffee in Brazil. An ordinary person from one person's perspective is an extraordinary person from another's.

And Patrick Swayze. Miracle bringer. Light bearer. Peaceful warrior. Special and precious soul. Thank you. May the paths of those you continue to touch be always safe and blessed. Rest sometimes.

Thank you. Thank you for reading.

ABOUT THE AUTHOR

Jodie Archer is a writer and medium. She has BA and MA degrees from the University of Cambridge, a Ph.D. from Stanford University, a BSc from the International University of Metaphysics, and her second Ph.D., this time in Metaphysical Science, is due in 2018. Jodie's other books include *Dancer* and *The Bestseller Code* (with Matthew L. Jockers), and *Coast-to-Coast* is forthcoming.

Visit Jodie at www.jodiearcher.com and www.archerjockers.com

Made in the USA
San Bernardino, CA
04 February 2018